# WOLVES
## FROM
# NIAGARA

## BUTLER'S RANGERS
### 1777-1784

*Mike Phifer*

HERITAGE BOOKS
2007

# HERITAGE BOOKS
*AN IMPRINT OF HERITAGE BOOKS, INC.*

**Books, CDs, and more—Worldwide**

For our listing of thousands of titles see our website
at
www.HeritageBooks.com

Published 2007 by
HERITAGE BOOKS, INC.
Publishing Division
65 East Main Street
Westminster, Maryland 21157-5026

International Standard Book Number: 978-0-7884-4319-4

To my Ranger ancestors - Averhart, Andrew, Peter, Job and Christian Barkley

# TABLE OF CONTENTS

# PREFACE

"This chosen corps - this band of brothers - was rarely worsted in any skirmish or action, though often obliged to retire and betake themselves to the wilderness when a superior force came against them. Sir John's Corps and Butler's rangers were very distressing to the back settlers; their advances and retreats were equally sudden and astonishing, and to this day the Americans say they might have as easily found out a parcel of wolves in the woods as them if they once entered it, that the first notice they had of their approach was them in sight, and of their retreat their being out of reach . . . I have known many of them both officers and soldiers, and the account they gave of the fatigue and suffering they underwent is hard credible, were it not confirmed by and all of them."
- Captain Patrick Campbell of the 42$^{nd}$ Royal Highland Regiment.

Campbell in one paragraph accurately summarizes the adventurous seven years Butler's Rangers were in operation. They were the best fighting Provincial unit serving in the Northern Department of the British Army. Ranging from the frontiers of New York to Kentucky, along with their Indian allies, the Rangers struck the Rebel settlements destroying food supplies that could be sent east to aid Washington's army as well as creating such a ruckus that troops desperately needed elsewhere would be forced to stay and protect the frontier. The suffering the Rangers underwent and the suffering they inflicted on their enemies is a fascinating chapter in the frontier war of America's first civil war. For over 20 years the story of Butler's Rangers has fascinated me and I'm quite pleased to tell a general history of their deeds. Most of the information for this book comes from secondary sources, much of it from the prolific chronicler of early Canadian history Ernest Cruikshank, whose works contains a wealth of first hand information.

Mike Phifer

# CHAPTER 1:
## THE 'DISAFFECTED'
### 1774 - 1776

When war finally broke out between the American colonies and England, it was more than a war of independence. It was an Indian war and a bloody civil war that tore family and neighbor asunder. This was particularly true for the frontier inhabitants of New York especially along the Mohawk Valley and Pennsylvania where most of the recruits would come from who enlisted in Butler's Rangers.

Those who chose to remain loyal, be it for loyalty to the crown, the draw of bounty and promise of land for military service to the King, fear of 'mob' rule, family and clan or ethnic ties, or for whatever reason, paid a hefty price in the persecution they and their family would suffer for the duration of the war.[1]

The Committee of Safety was formed by the Patriots during the war to match and eventually supplant Crown officials. Any who spoke ill of the Continental Congress, showed any loyalty to the Crown, helped fleeing Loyalists, aiding the enemy or generally running afoul of the Committee for whatever reason could find themselves paid a visit by the Committee. The offender would be coerced to sign an 'association' which among other things obligated the signer to support the Patriot cause, boycott British goods and generally behave themselves. They could also be fined, have all interaction cut off, banished or if the offender was deemed dangerous they could end up in an overcrowded jail. Worse, an offender could be sent to the infamous Simsbury Mines. It was an abandoned copper mine converted into a prison, where the offender was placed 70 feet underground in a damp dark shaft with little food or air. Sickness, ill health and death awaited anybody cooped up in that mine for any length of time. A more 'obnoxious' repeat dangerous offender could possibly expect a hangman's noose.[2]

In this atmosphere of suspicion, intimation and persecution that prevailed, Loyalists began to find life uncomfortable on the New York and Pennsylvania frontier. Besides apprehension of the Committee of Safety, and neighbors who might inform the Committee of the Loyalist's behavior, true or possibly to settle an old grudge, there was the mob to fear. Tar and feathering, beatings, riding the rail and lynching were all real possibilities.

Loyalist leaders soon found themselves in conflict with the Committee of Safety early in the war. Sir John Johnson, son of the late Sir William Johnson and inheritor of his vast land holdings and a large number of Highland Scot tenants in the Mohawk Valley, had a run in with the Rebels when they attempted to raise a liberty pole in May of 1775. Sir John, his cousin Guy Johnson, brother-in-law Daniel Claus, neighbor John Butler along with some of his tenants had a scuffle with the Rebels. Fearful of the Johnsons and the sway they had with the Mohawks and other Iroquois tribes, the Rebel inhabitants of the Valley and the Committee would spar with them until finally Guy left the Valley with a large group of followers. Sir John who had fortified his estate and armed his Scottish tenants, (mostly McDonnells who had come from Scotland to take up their tenant farms in New York in 1773) were forced to give up their guns by a large Patriot force and promised not to take up arms against Congress. Twelve men were taken hostage to ensure good behavior by the Rebels. This was not the end. Sir John was again under suspicion and eventually the order came for his arrest. With 170 people, Sir John fled north through the Adirondacks to Canada, where he would raise a Loyalist regiment.[3]

While Sir John headed through the wilderness, his wife unable to accompany him because of her pregnancy was left alone with his two young children. They were quickly arrested by the Rebels, but would manage to escape later to the British at New York City. John Butler also had his wife and some of his children arrested by the Rebels and would not see them for much of the war. Many of the Loyalists who were forced to flee the frontier for the British at Fort Niagara or elsewhere left their families behind in hopes they would be left alone. They were wrong as seen with Lady Johnson and

Catherine Butler. The Patriots arrested many Loyalists women in hopes to ensure good behavior from their husbands and kin.

Many women left behind helped the Loyalist cause by sending information and aiding raiding parties. Sarah Kast McGinnis for example, had close ties with the Mohawk, her husband having been an Indian trader and Indian Department agent until he was killed in the French and Indian War. During the Revolution, Sarah, her daughter and granddaughter were arrested by the Committee of Safety and roughly treated. Sarah's granddaughter would eventually die from the ill treatment. The Rebels tried to recruit Sarah to their side and use her persuasion with the Mohawk to their benefit, but she refused. Sarah and her daughter were temporarily released and fled to Canada before the Rebels could recapture them. In Montreal, she was recruited by the British to return to Iroquois country to ensure their loyalty and forward intelligence through the Indians to them.

For other Loyalist women and children left behind they could have their property confiscated because of their husbands going off to fight for the Crown. Physical abuse and robbery were very real fears for these women and children left alone amongst unfriendly Rebel neighbors. Other women and children headed to Canada for safety.[4]

The men who made their way through Iroquois country to Fort Niagara were anxious to get back into the war and revisit their Rebel neighbors. They would soon have their chance. By 1777, a Loyalist ranger unit was being raised under the command of John Butler to fight with the Indians.

By 1775, John Butler had spent most of his adult live in the Mohawk Valley and knew well the intricacies of Indian diplomacy. Born in 1728 in New London, Connecticut, John came to the Valley fourteen years later with his mother and siblings to join his father, Captain Walter Butler, who had purchased land across the Mohawk River from his posting at Fort Hunter. Not long after arriving on the New York frontier, young John found employment along with his brothers, Thomas and Walter Jr. in the Indian Department under the wealthy and influential William Johnson, a friend of John's father, who by 1756 was the Superintendent of Northern Indian affairs. John acted as an interpreter at a grand council held at Mount Johnson in June of 1755 to recruit Iroquois for the war against the French.

Serving as a lieutenant in the Indian Department, John along with his brother, Walter Jr. accompanied an expedition of 3,000 Provincial soldiers and 300 Indians led by Johnson to capture fort Saint-Frederic (Crown Point, New York) on Lake Champlain. Encamped at Lake George, a large scouting force was ambushed by the French and their Indian allies on September 8, 1755. The scouting force was routed back to the encampment where the French attacked the rest of Johnson's army. In the bloody battle the French and Indians were repulsed. Although the expedition was eventually canceled, William Johnson was made a baronet for the victory. Sadness was John's reward for the battle as his brother Walter Jr. was killed.

John eventually became a captain in the Indian Department taking part in the failed British and Provincial expedition against Fort Carillon (Fort Ticonderoga, New York) as well as the successful capture of Fort Frontenac (Kingston, Ontario) both in 1758. The following year acting as second in command of the Indians, John was present at the siege of Fort Niagara. When the British commander was accidently killed, Sir William took over command of the British and Provincial army while Butler took charge of the large Indian contingent. After a French and Indian relief force was ambushed, the commandant of Fort Niagara surrendered to Johnson.

In 1760, again acting as second in command to Johnson, Butler was with General Amherst's army that moved down the St. Lawrence River, capturing Fort Levis (near Prescott, Ontario) as they advanced on Montreal to join to other British and Provincial armies moving in from the south and east. With the fall of Montreal, the war in North America essentially ended, although official peace would not come until 1763 with the Treaty of Paris which succeeded Canada to the British.

In 1752, John had married Catharine Bradt and together they had four sons and a daughter that lived, two of their children having died in infancy. With the war over John had more time to spend with his family on his 3,400 estate at Butlersbury (near Johnstown, New York) left to him by his father who had died in 1760. With his ability to speak various Iroquois dialects John continued to work occasionally as an interpreter in the British Indian Department. Much of Butler's time was now devoted to his growing estate which would eventually expand to 26,600 acres making him the second wealthiest man, next to Sir William, in the Valley. John was appointed as justice of the peace and by 1772 became a justice of the Court of Quarter Sessions for the recently created Tryon County. He also became lieutenant-colonel in the Tryon militia regiment commanded by Sir William's nephew, Guy Johnson.[5]

## CHAPTER 2:
## RACE FOR THE INDIAN FAVOR
## 1775 - 1776

When words turned to bullets at Lexington and Concord, both sides - Patriot and British - knew the Indians would be an important factor in the conflict. In the Mohawk Valley, John Butler found himself playing a major role in the British Indian Department again. In 1774, Sir William had died and Guy Johnson took over as Superintendent of Indian Affairs.

As both sides began to court the Iroquois Confederacy (also called the Six Nations and made up of the Mohawk, Oneida, Onondaga, Cayuga, Tuscarora and Seneca tribes), Guy Johnson intended on having a large Indian council. On May 31, 1775 he led a large contingent of 120 whites and 90 Mohawks upriver toward Fort Stanwix (Rome, New York.) on May 31, 1775. Accompanying him, besides his wife and children, was Daniel Claus and his family, Joseph Brant, John Butler and his son Walter. When Johnson reached Fort Stanwix, he did not have enough Indian presents and with no chance of getting them from New York due to the Rebels, he sent off runners with request for supplies from Fort Niagara, Oswegatchie (Ogdensburg, New York)on the St. Lawrence River and Montreal.

From Governor Guy Carleton at Montreal he also requested 200 soldiers for he found the Oneida's alliance shaky. Missionary and Patriot Samuel Kirkland had some sway over the Oneidas and had managed to convince them to stay neutral, although he was trying to swing them and the other Iroquois tribes over to the Rebel side. Johnson was trying to swing the Iroquois to the British side. Before leaving to hold the Indian council, Johnson had received a message

15

from Major General Thomas Gage, commander in chief of British forces in North America, in besieged Boston to recruit as many Indians as he could and take them to Montreal where he was to join with Carleton in an attack on the Rebels on the New England frontier.

Moving on, Guy Johnson arrived at the crumbling ruins of Fort Ontario at Oswego located on the east shore of Lake Ontario on June 17. Their food and guns reached him from Fort Niagara just in time for the council he conducted. Over 1,450 Indians showed up, mostly from the Six Nations, but also a few Hurons as well. John Butler no doubt was busy interpreting during the conference. For Guy Johnson the conference was not a big success. Although the Indians in attendance proved to be amicable to the Crown, most still preferred to remain neutral.[6]

With 220 warriors and whites, Guy Johnson headed for Montreal on July 11. It was a sad trip for him, as his wife died in childbirth just prior to the party pushing off in their bateaus and sloop. Among the whites, were John and Walter Butler who again would be involved in another Indian council Guy Johnson conducted in late July at Montreal. Over 1,700 Caughnawagas, Seven Nations of Canada and Mississaugas attended with mixed results. Guy Johnson managed to recruit some of their warriors, but Johnson was restrained by Carleton how they would be used.

Regardless of Guy Johnson's orders from Gage, Carleton wanted the Indians to only serve in the defense of Canada. Five hundred warriors encamped near Montreal, who had agreed to fight, soon saw service when a Rebel army moved up the Richelieu River and besieged Fort St. Johns (Quebec). Walter Butler was involved in the fighting around St. Johns and helped capture Ethan Allen on his rash attack on Montreal.

In September, Daniel Claus, Deputy Superintendent to the Canadian Indians, received a shock when he was dismissed and replaced by Major John Campbell. Carleton approved the change and quickly informed Guy Johnson he had no authority over the Canadian Indians either. Carleton wanted Guy to handle Indian affairs out of Fort Niagara. Guy had other ideas. He was going to England to secure his own position. In his absence he asked John Butler to go to Fort Niagara and act as his agent in dealing with the Iroquois. Butler would have preferred to return to the Mohawk Valley and see to the welfare of his family, but agreed to go if Guy would petition the government in granting Butler to be a deputy in the British Indian Department.

While Guy Johnson, Daniel Claus, and other Indian Department employees such as Gilbert Tice and Joseph Chew sailed for England, John Butler headed upriver for Fort Niagara. Carleton was grateful for John Butler's service, but had only contempt for Johnson and Claus. Carleton saw their leaving as deserting especially with the Rebels advancing into Canada. Accompanying Johnson and Claus was Walter Butler who carried with him a recommendation from Carleton to obtain a commission in the regular army. Joseph Brant also went.

On November 17, John Butler arrived at Fort Niagara and set up his office in the trader's quarters located between the Niagara River and the stone walls of the fort. John's position as an agent was unenviable one for he found himself serving two masters - Guy Johnson and Governor Carleton whose jurisdiction included Fort Niagara as well the purse strings for the Indian Department. Both men had opposing views on the use of Indians in the war and John found himself receiving contradictory orders from them. Johnson wanted to turn the Indians loose on the frontier, while Carleton preferred securing the Indians to the King's side but limiting their use for the time being. Often Butler would lean more to Carleton's wishes as this was the more realistic of the two and more to John's personal persuasion.

John Butler's task of trying to keeping the Iroquois neutral for now, but loyal to the Crown became even more difficult when worded reached Niagara that Montreal had fallen to the Patriots in November. As long as the Rebels held Montreal, supplies including Indian presents were shut off from reaching Fort Niagara. To make matters worse, Patriot agents had moved into Indian country were having some success in encouraging the Iroquois to move away from their support of the King.

With his work cut out for him, Butler tackled it with zeal. The Mohawks tended to be strongly in favor of the King, while the Oneidas and Tuscaroras favored the Rebels. The remaining three nations - Senecas, Onondagas and Cayugas had not sided with anybody yet. In the spring of 1776, John began conducting councils with the Six Nations, especially the three undecided tribes. In a council with the Indians, Butler pointed out the weakness of the

Rebels in guns, cannons, clothing and their inability to give the Indian presents. The King, he reminded them, had an abundance of everything they could desire. He liberally distributed presents and rum to the Indians despite the fort's dwindling supplies.

Ships laden with food arrived from Detroit with the spring thaw to alleviate the hunger that stalked the garrison of Fort Niagara. Montreal was still in the hands of the Patriots blocking all supplies from coming from that direction. Butler attempted to raise Iroquois warriors to join an expedition under Captain Forester stationed at Oswegatchie to strike the Rebels at Montreal from the west. Unfortunately he had little success in getting their aid as they still clung to their stated neutrality. He managed to recruit only about 50 warriors who left with a handful of Indian Department officers for Oswegatchie to join Forester on May 10 arriving two days later. These warriors along with Mississaugas, British and French traders and a company of the 8th's Light Infantry took a Rebel post at the Cedars on the St. Lawrence River and defeated a relief column taking over 500 prisoners.[7]

Forester moved on toward Montreal which he decided was too strong and pulled back to Oswegatchie at the end of May. The Rebel force however, were soon driven out of Montreal by British troops moving upriver from Quebec City after having first arrived from England. Canada and the St. Lawrence River were back in the hands of the British now allowing supply laden bateaus to be rowed upriver to Oswegatchie where the supplies were transferred to ships for the journey onto Fort Niagara.

Butler meanwhile continued to try and secure Seneca support, by speaking with many of the various tribes leaders both civil and war. He had a council with them, along with a few Shawnee from May 31 to June 7. He admonished them not to believe the things told them by the Rebels last year at a council at Pittsburgh for they met to cheat them warned Butler. If the Indians did take the Rebels advice continued Butler and should the Rebels defeat "the King's Army, their intention is to take all your Lands from you and destroy your people . . .." He then urged them to take up the hatchet against the Rebels.

After two days of council among themselves their representative told Butler that he was "mad, foolish, crazy and a deceitful person." The Seneca chief continued by telling him that the

Americans were the wise people as they told them to "sit still" since the war was "between yourselves."[8]

Butler had a Mohawk the next day in council rebuke the warriors who were leaning to the Rebels. A war chief of the Seneca responded the following day by telling Butler "they had lived in Peace" with the Americans for a long time and they would continue to due so as long as possible. "When they hurt us it is time to strike them," he added. They would speak with the Patriots encroaching on their land. He also pointed out to Butler that if they were so strong and the Americans weak, why did they need their assistance.[9] Despite the poor results of the council, Butler did manage to convince about 30 Senecas to take up the hatchet and head to Canada and attack the Rebels already in retreat.

While Butler did his best to cajole the Seneca to the Crown's side, Congress had decided to change their strategy of fostering Indian neutrality to attempt to raise an Indian force to aid them in their revolution. The Oneidas and Tuscaroras by the end of May were moving away from their neutrality and heading more firmly to the Patriot side. This civil war was not only among the whites.

By the end of July of 1776, both Guy Johnson and Joseph Brant were back from England. They arrived at the British controlled Staten Island. With him, Johnson carried his commission as Superintendent of Indian Affairs with the same power his uncle, Sir William, had. However, Guy authority did not cover the Canadian Indians.

After the Rebel's defeat at Long Island and retreat from New York City, the British took control of the city. Guy Johnson remained in the city, while he ordered Brant and Gilbert Tice to head into Indian country, make a wampum belt and to recruit Indian to "the King's Service."[10] After stopping at his home village of Oquaga to visit his wife and family, Brant and a small party pushed onto Fort Niagara, stopping at villages along the way preaching and urging the Indians to join the British side in the war.

After arriving at Niagara, Brant informed Butler of his activities and requested some gunpowder. A reserved Butler gave him very little and reviewed Johnson's message with restraint and was not overly cooperative. What Brant planned was in contradiction what Butler's orders were from Carleton.

Brant left Niagara with hard feeling toward Butler and set out to recruit warriors. He sent a message to the Canadian Iroquois at Akwesasne and Kanehsatake asking them to join in an expedition in the spring where they could fight their own way and not serve under 'regular troops.' Carleton was horrified when he got wind of Brant's message fearing he met to lead "an indiscriminate attack" which would see women, children and the elderly "exposed" to the Indian's fury. Carleton quickly ordered Butler and Canadian Indian Department agents to foil Brant's plan which they did.[11] It would not be long though, before Butler would be recruiting warriors for a coming military expedition.

# CHAPTER 3:
## ST. LEGER'S EXPEDITION
### 1777

On May 6, 1777, Major General John Burgoyne arrived in Quebec with a Grand Strategy to end the rebellion by slicing New England from the rest of colonies. Burgoyne was to lead a large army of British regulars, Hessians, Loyalists and Indians south from Montreal, along Lake Champlain and onto Albany. There another army under the command General William Howe moving up the Hudson River from New York City would meet him along with a smaller diversionary force moving east from Oswego through the Mohawk Valley. This force, made up mostly of Loyalists, Indians and a handful of regulars and German Jagers was under the command Lieutenant-Colonel Barry St. Leger who breveted to Brigadier-General for this expedition. With the three forces combined, a string of posts would be built from Montreal to New York City which would isolate New England and quell the rebellion where is started.[12]

A month later, June 5, Butler received orders from Carleton to gather as many warriors as he could from the Six Nations, as well as from any other tribes and join St. Leger's expedition.[13] Butler quickly sent runners to the Six Nations and even to some Mississaugas to assemble at Irondequoit Bay. Butler on June 15, according to orders, sent a list of his recommended officers and their rate of pay, along with a list of his Indian Department Rangers to Carleton. The list included 14 officers and 75 rangers. He also requested to be given the rank of Lieutenant-Colonel.

Butler arrived at Irondequoit bay on July 13 and began a week long council three days later. An abundance of provisions, food and rum was lavished on the Senecas when they arrived overwhelming them with the King's abundances. When the council commenced Butler reminded the Iroquois of their ancient alliance with the crown and urged them to help the King defeat the Rebels. By agreeing to do so, the Iroquois would be well rewarded. Although some sections of the Senecas, especially those of the Allegheny and Genesee settlements, were loyal to the crown, the Seneca sections located closes to the Patriot missionaries along with the Oneidas and Tuscarora preferred to remain neutral. It was decided by their leaders after a lengthy discussion that they would stay out of the war.

Despite this setback, Butler continued to remind the Senecas of the British strength and their ample supply of rum. He also assured them their families would be well looked after and they would want for nothing. For a day and half the Senecas conducted an intense debate amongst themselves what they should do. Not waiting for the Seneca to come a decision, Butler showered an unheard amount of beads, ostrich feathers and other gewgaws on them.

After the council recommenced, Butler showed two wampum belts, one of which was the Great Old Covenant Chain - a visual reminder to their old alliance with the Crown. After discussing things again, the Senecas agreed to accompany the expedition and appointed two war captains - Sayengaraghta (also called Old Smoke) and Cornplanter, a mixed blood Seneca. At great feast was held where each important warrior was given a gun, powder, lead, a hatchet and a knife. The promise of a bounty for prisoners or scalps was also made.[14]

On July 20, Butler dispatched 150 warriors to join an "alert" against Fort Stanwix as spelled out in an order from St. Leger received the day before. Fort Stanwix, which had been built in the French and Indian War and protected the western approach to the Mohawk Valley, also guarded the Great Carrying Place, the portage located between the Mohawk River and the Wood Creek which led to Lake Ontario.[15] The fort lay square in St. Leger's path.

Butler arrived at Oswego with a large number of Indians on July 25 to a very unpleasant surprise. Daniel Claus he was quickly informed would be in charge of the Indians. A letter from Carleton proved Claus's seniority. This must have been a bitter disappointment for John Butler especially since Claus disliked him.

More bad news greeted Butler. The Indian presents and

supplies he has sent ahead to Oswego had been handed out by Claus to Joseph Brant and the 300 warriors with him. Butler needed these presents to give the Indians at a conference he was planning to hold. No conference would be held here at Oswego he was informed by Claus. The warriors coming for the council had been ordered to wait at Three Rivers by Claus as it was closer to Fort Stanwix. Indians on the warpath did not expect "formal Meetings and counselling" lectured Claus to Butler adding it would delay their advance by a few days.[16] The veteran Indian agent was shocked by Claus's ignorance of the shaky alliance. The Indians had come to a council not necessarily to go on a military campaign. Butler was going to try to persuade them to do so, but now Claus had jeopardized that with his interference.

As the expedition moved toward the Fort Stanwix, Butler held an Indian conference at Three Rivers. Claus, who in charge of the Indians, was absent from this important treaty. War belts were handed out to the various tribes. Joseph Brant accepted for the Mohawks then quickly left the council for Fort Stanwix. Other Mohawk war leaders took the belt as well, although some Mohawks fearing for the safety of their family living close to the Rebels in the Fort Hunter and Canajoharie area remained neutral. Cornplanter and Sayengaraghta accepted the war belt for the Seneca. The Onondagas and Cayugas were divided with only half accepting the war belt. With the aid of rum and presents, Butler had managed a fairly successful council.[17]

The "alert," consisting of 30 men of the 8th King's Regiment under Lieutenant Henry Bird, as well 200 warriors led by Brant, a chief named Bull along with two Indian Department officers - Captain John Hare and Captain James Wilson, object was to capture the landing place below the fort and cut of communications with the settlements. It was hoped this move might cause the garrison to surrender. Bird arrived a hair's breadth too late to intercept a brigade of boats loaded with ammunition and supplies, which were quickly taken inside the fort.

A day later, August 3, elements of St. Leger's army arrived (St. Leger himself had arrived the evening before). His force, part of which was still making its way up Wood Creek, consisted of detachments from the 34th Regiment, 8th King's Regiment, a company of Jagers (the rest of the battalion hurrying the St. Lawrence

River to catch up), the King's Royal Regiment of New York, Indian Department Rangers, light artillery and a company of Canadian militia. In total it numbered around 875. The Indians numbered around a 1,000.[18]

Fort Stanwix was much stronger than what St. Leger had been led to believe as he later reported to Carleton: "The accounts we received in Canada concerning Fort Stanwix were the most erroneous that can be conceived. Instead of the unsuitable and unfinished work we were taught to expect, I found it a respectable fortress strongly garrisoned with 700 men and a train of artillery we were not masters of for its speedy subjection."[19] The fort was ordered to surrender, which the commander, Colonel Peter Gansesvoort, refused.

For the next two days, St. Leger's men occupied themselves by cutting a road from Wood Creek to be able to bring up their artillery and supplies. Then a crucial message arrived from Molly Brant, widow of Sir William Johnson and sister to Joseph Brant, who was living at Canajoharie. Eight hundred Rebels of the Tryon militia under General Nicholas Herkimer were on their way to the fort. On July 30, after hearing of St. Leger invading force, Herkimer had ordered the militia to gather at Fort Dayton which was located 30 miles below Fort Stanwix along the Mohawk River. On August 4, the militia, along with their train of oxcarts and wagons set out to raise the siege.[20]

With his army spread out building roads, St. Leger chose not to wait to be attacked fearing that a force would sally out of the fort and attack him in the rear as Herkimer attacked his front. St. Leger ordered Butler, who had just arrived from the conference at Three Rivers, to take his Indian Department Rangers and as many Indians as he could get and intercept Herkimer's force. Sir John Johnson urged that he be given command of this force and be allowed to take his light company as well. St. Leger agreed.[21]

Butler managed to rally about 500 Indians, many of them being with Brant, but there was a significant number of Seneca, Cayuga, Mohawks and Onondagas, as well as 50 or so Lake Indians. The white force numbered about 80 men.[22] It was 5 P.M. when Johnson's force moved out making about five miles that evening, before they stopped for the night.

Scouts returned the next morning, August 6, with information that Herkimer was only a few miles away. Butler, as well as Johnson, hoped to avoid a battle with the hope that the Tryon militia would lay down their arms or disperse. This was civil war; Loyalist against Patriot, brother against brother, and it was hoped by them, since families were divided, some of the militia might be friendly and a fight could be avoided. Butler proposed a summons should be sent to the militia to lay down their arms and go home. Brant would have nothing of it, arguing that chance of surprise would be gone as well as the fact that the militia was already armed and on the march and that the time for peace overtures was over. Brant's opinion triumphed and the Rangers, light infantrymen and Indians moved out to choose a site for an ambush.[23]

The area chosen was about 6 miles east of Fort Stanwix, where a wagon road surrounded by forest dipped into a deep ravine and crossed a marsh by way of a log causeway near Oriskany Creek. Sir John Johnson and his light company took up position on the crest of the western slope, across the road to check the movement of the militia. Later they would be reinforced by a handful of Jagers. The Rangers and Indians took cover in the trees and brush on the flanks of the road with orders to gain the rear of the militia column once the attack began. The ambush formed a giant U along the wagon road. All there was now for Butler, Johnson and Brant to do was wait for Herkimer to march into the open end of the U.

There was trouble in the Patriot militia camp on the morning of August 6. Herkimer was worried about what St. Leger was up to and advised caution. The previous night he had sent four men to try and get to Fort Stanwix and warn Gansevoort that a relief force was on the way and for him to make a sortie to distract St. Leger. Gansevoort was to fire three cannon shots to confirm the plan; so far there had been no reply. Colonel Ebenezer Cox, commander of the 1st Regiment of Tryon militia was anxious to getting moving and was not shy in voicing his opinion. Many other officers agreed with him, with attacks on Herkimer's courage and comments on the fact that Herkimer's brother was serving in the British Indian Department with St. Leger. Herkimer gave in and the army moved out. Herkimer did take some comfort that last night 60 Oneidas had joined him and now acted as scouts.[24]

The militia was divided into four regiments with Colonel Cox leading off, followed by Colonel Jacob Klock's 2nd Regiment, next came the Oneidas and the brigade staff with Colonel Peter Bellinger's

4th Regiment behind them. Colonel Richard Visscher's 3rd Regiment was split with companies in front of the 15 creaking wagons packed with supplies and baggage and the rest of the regiment behind them.[25] It was 10 A.M. in the morning when they entered the ravine and the trap.

As Cox and Herkimer, who was riding ahead of the 1st Regiment, were heading up the west side of the ravine, the ambush was sprung - but too soon. Some of the Indians were impatient and did not wait for Visscher to march into the trap. A vicious volley was let loose by the Indians and Loyalist staggering the militia column and dropping men in droves. Herkimer, turning his horse around took a rifle ball just below his knee and another ball killed his horse. Cox trying to rally his men was killed shortly afterward. To the rear of the column Visscher's companies following the wagons, which were now overrun by Brant's men, seeing the carnage before them, fled with the Indians in pursuit.[26]

As the initial shock wore off, the militia began to return fire. They were still taking heavy casualties by the Indians who "made a shocking slaughter among them with their spears and hatchets" wrote Butler in his report to Governor Carleton. "The rebels," Butler would go on to write, "however, recovering themselves, fell back to a more advantageous ground . . . ."[27] Fighting their way up to higher ground, the Rebels formed a rough circle between two ravines. Herkimer was taken and set underneath a tree on his saddle in the center of his men where he could give orders.

The fighting continued when suddenly dark clouds opened and pelted the combatants with heavy rain and a thunderstorm. The killing temporarily ceased as each side waited out the storm. The Rebels took advantage of the intermission to tighten their defences and reorganize. Johnson quickly headed back to the main camp and reported to St. Leger what had happened and to get more reinforcements. Captain-Lieutenant Donald John McDonell's company of the King's Royal Regiment of New York was ordered into the foray.

Three canon shots could be heard booming from Fort Stanwix indicating that a sortie was on its way as requested by Herkimer in the message he had sent to the fort. John Butler also knew the meaning of the cannon shots, having got the information from a prisoner. With this knowledge he decided to give the Rebels a surprise. With the arrival of McDonell's men, Butler had them turn their green coats inside out so they now appeared greyish. Butler hoped the militia would think McDonell's men were a relief force from Stanwix.

As the rain slackened, the Rebels could see a column of men marching down the road toward them. They wore gray coats and not the green of the Loyalists so they had to be reinforcements from Fort Stanwix who had come to their rescue. A cheer rose up from the bloodied and powder-stained militia.

Captain Gardiner of the 4th Regiment perceived something was wrong when suddenly he realized the column coming was not Continentals - but Tories. He warned his men, but no one paid heed to him. One of the militia men jumped to his feet and rushed toward the column. He was quickly grabbed by the Loyalists and pulled inside their ranks and made a prisoner. Gardiner had seen enough. With spontoon in his hand he charged the enemy to free the prisoner. Three Loyalists went after Gardiner, bayoneting him in the calf of each leg and pinning him to the ground. The third Loyalist went for the chest. Gardiner grabbed the bayonet with his hand and pulled the Loyalist on top of him and used him as a shield. By this time a militia man had rushed into the scuffle and helped Gardiner to his feet. In a rage Gardiner grabbed a spontoon and drove it into the Loyalist wounding him.

The militia still held their fire, until Gardiner returned and ordered them to shoot. The fighting became savage as Tory fought Rebel. Suddenly an Indian messenger arrived with news a sortie from Fort Stanwix had attacked their camps. Lieutenant-Colonel Marinus Willet, second in command of Fort Stanwix, with 250 men and a field piece attacked St. Leger's camp. He looted their encampments, especially the Indian's camp, and returned to the fort, heavily laden with captured goods. Captain Hoyes led men from the 34th and 8th to attack Willet, but the damage was already done.

"Oonah" cried the Indians as their signal to fall back and return to their camps. With the loss of their Indian allies, the Loyalist troops had no choice but to withdraw has well. Despite withdrawing, Butler and Johnson had done their job - the relief force was stopped.

Out of 800 militia men, 500 were killed, wounded or missing. Herkimer had little option but to turn around and head home. In a few days Herkimer would be dead too; the surgeon being unable to stop the bleeding from what was left of Herkimer's leg after it was amputated. The Loyalist casualties were light: 3 killed and 3 wounded. The Indians on the other hand suffered 33 killed and 29 wounded, about half who were Senecas. This was considered heavy casualties in the Indian's idea of waging war.[28]

In the following days after the ambush, the siege went on. Johnson urged St. Leger to allow him take 200 men and a "sufficient body of men" under Daniel Claus and strike the Mohawk Valley. With the heavy losses the Tryon militia had taken at Oriskany it was believed the Rebels could be broken in the Valley. St. Leger refused claiming he could not spare the troops from the siege.[29] Possibly he feared the havoc and vengeance the Loyalists and Indians would unleash on the Rebel inhabitants of the valley.

On August 8, Butler, along with Captain William Ancrum, a British officer, and a doctor headed toward the fort under a flag of truce. With them they had terms of surrender from their commander which threatened the garrison that if they did not capitulate, St. Leger would be unable to control the large number of Indians from not only plundering the garrison, but killing most of them as well.[30] They also warned that the Indians in retaliation for the losses they suffered at Oriskany including some of their favourite chiefs might ravage the valley killing men, women and children. Gansevoort said he would have an answer the next morning.

At 1 A.M., Willet and another man, slipped out of the fort and through St. Leger's lines and made their way down the valley to warn to inhabitants and rally the remains of the Tryon militia after their recent mauling. After a few exchanged letters, Gansevoort declared the fort would not surrender. The siege, which was temporarily halted for the surrender negotiations, continued again.

On August 13, it was decided by Johnson, Butler and Claus to send a proclamation by St. Leger as well one by themselves and a third one to the inhabitants of the valley urging them to support the King. John Butler's son, Walter, now an ensign in the 8th Regiment was to take ten British troops, along with two Indian Department officers, two Loyalist soldiers and three Iroquois warriors under a flag of truce and deliver the message to the valley inhabitants. After reaching German Flats two days later, Walter let it be known that he was at Shoemaker's Inn and would have important news that night to give to the inhabitants. Walter was quickly arrested with the rest of his party on August 17. A court martial was ordered by Major-General Benedict Arnold, who was leading a relief force to break the siege of Fort Stanwix. Willet was to act as Judge advocate, while Walter, a lawyer by trade, defended himself. Young Butler was charged as a traitor and a spy who under the guise of a flag of truce was attempting to entice "the inhabitants of this state from their allegiance to the United States of America."[31]

Three days later the court martial began for Walter who pled not guilty. The court however saw things differently. Walter was found guilty and sentenced to hang. One of the two loyalists soldiers accompanying Butler, was sentenced to 100 lashes while the other was sentenced to be put to death (whether he was or not is unknown). One of the Indian Department officers, Peter Ten Broeck cooperated with the court and managed to save his own neck. The British soldiers were considered prisoners of war. The Indians were held prisoner as well.[32]

The light artillery brought along by St. Leger was proving ineffective against the fort's walls. The mortars were not doing much either. If a breach was to be made, a mine would have to be dug and extended underneath a bastion of the fort, filled with black powder and set off. It was not to be. Arnold's force at Fort Dayton which had grown to 950 men, many who were Continentals, were about to break the siege.

Arnold decided to use covert activity to weaken the determination of the Indians. Hon Yost Schulyer, a Loyalist prisoner who had been sentenced to death for attempting to recruit for the British, was offered a pardon by Arnold. If Hon Yost wanted to live, he would have to journey to St. Leger's camp and spread stories to the Indians of Arnold's large force advancing toward them. Hon Yost agreed and even had his coat fired on to make it bullet ridden and look like he made a narrow escape. The Indians were alarmed at Hon Yost's news, which became more believable when a pro-Rebel Oneida arrived in camp and spread the same stories of Arnold's army which was said to number anywhere from 1,000 to 3,000 men.

St. Leger, along with Butler, Claus and Johnson tried to calm the Indians, but it was too late. Two hundred of them had already left and the rest insisted on a retreat. St. Leger's told them he would "retire at night." "This did not fall in with their views," St. Leger reported, "which were no less than treacherously committing ravage upon their friends as they had lost the opportunity of doing it upon their Enemies . . .."[33] The Indians began falsely reporting that the enemy was close, which caused a panic in the camp. St. Leger's retreated, leaving behind tents, supplies and artillery. To make matters worse the Indians began plundering the British camp. The siege and campaign fell apart on August 22. Arnold arrived at Fort Stanwix the following day to the cheers of the defenders.

By August 26, St. Leger's army had reached Oswego where the commander held a council with his senior officers to discuss the next course of events. Most of his officers were for heading back to Fort Stanwix, while St. Leger preferred to retire back to Montreal, resupply and join Burgoyne. Butler was ordered to go to Montreal, instead of returning to Niagara, to get presents for the discontent Indians. The Indians, especially those closest to the whites settlements feared Rebel retaliation which did occur for the Fort Hunter Mohawks.[34]

In mid-September Butler, along with three Iroquois chiefs arrived at Quebec City. There Butler introduced the chiefs to Carleton who informed the Governor of their wish to see troops at Oswego to be able to aid them from Rebel attacks. Butler who spoke privately with Carleton proposed to raise a corps of rangers to serve with the Indians if the Governor with give him a beating order. Carleton agreed. Butler's Rangers was born.

The Rangers were to consist of eight companies, two of which were to be made up of "people speaking the Indian language and acquainted with their customs and manner of making war." The other companies were "to be composed of people well acquainted with the woods, in consideration of the fatigue they are liable to undergo." Each company was to consist of a captain, a first and second lieutenant, three sergeants and three corporals along with fifty privates. The two companies acquainted with the Indian customs were to be paid 4 shillings New York Currency a day, while men in the other companies were to be paid to 2 shillings. Noncommissioned officers were to paid more, while officers were to be paid at same rate as officers "in his Majesty's service." Everybody was "to cloath and arm themselves at their own expense."[35]

Butler was then ordered by Carleton to take what Rangers he already raised and as many Iroquois or other Indians as he could and join Burgoyne. Claus could not have been happy to hear of John Butler's orders to lead an Indian contingent to aid Burgoyne. The news got worse for him when Carleton informed he was no longer needed in Indian Affairs. John Butler was now to look after Indian Affairs while Guy Johnson was absent. Claus who had ran up quite an expense for Indian presents would not have his accounts honoured by Carleton who disliked him. Butler on the other hand had all his expenses honoured by the Governor.[36]

By early November, Butler was back at Niagara. Before he could rally an Indian force to aid Burgoyne word reached him that Burgoyne's surrender on October 17. In December, a great council was held at Niagara with almost 3,000 Indians showing up from the Six Nations and other tribes. Butler, along with Colonel Mason Bolton, the new commander of Fort Niagara, downplayed Burgoyne's defeat reassuring the Indians the British were just beginning to fight. Large amount of presents and goods were given to the Indians to compensate for their losses with St. Leger.[37]

By mid-December, Butler had one company of rangers formed and soon as his recruiting officers returned, along with the refugees making their way to Fort Niagara, he hoped to have two more companies before long. After the failed siege of Fort Stanwix, a small band of Rangers under the command of Lieutenant James Secord had received permission to return home most of which was in the Wyoming Valley along the Susquehanna River in Pennsylvania. There they were to "fetch their families into Niagara" as well drive in cattle to the fort, but on January 3, 1778, they were taken prisoner by the Rebels in the Wyoming Valley. Of the 27 Rangers, 18 were sent to prison in Connecticut while the rest for want of evidence were released. They quickly made their way to Niagara.[38] They were not the only ones to come from that region. A fair number of recruits escaped persecution there and joined the Rangers. They would soon be returning to visit old neighbours.

## CHAPTER 4:
## "EVERY PARTY YOU SEND OUT TO BURN AND DESTROY EVERYTHING"
## 1778

The war now had changed for Butler's Rangers and their Indian allies. This year, 1778, they would not be accompanying large invading British armies, instead they would strike the back settlements, destroying crops, granaries, property and anything that would aid the enemy. They would carry off what supplies they needed. Supplying Fort Niagara and the other posts of the upper country was major undertaking for the British. Some of the food was brought in from Ireland. In the coming years supply problems would only get worse. Another key object was to harass the frontier and keep Rebel troops occupied there instead of fighting with Washington.

In late spring, Butler moved his force from Niagara into Indian country. A council was held at Kanadasaga were Butler met with the Senecas. Good news greeted John Butler here. His oldest son, Walter, who had been sentenced to hang after being captured by the Rebels, managed to escape from Albany where he was being held and made his way toward Fort Niagara. It was at Kanadasaga that father and son were reunited. Walter Butler, now a Captain in the Rangers, was ordered to go to Quebec and try to obtain arms and clothing for the Rangers. Many of the recruits joining the Rangers were "nearly destitute of clothing and necessaries," Walter would report, "and having no Bounty allowed them confirmed by the General they being obliged to buy their Arms brings them greatly in debt . . . ."[39] These new recruits new little of military drill, but in the words of Governor Haldimand, who replaced Carleton as governor of

Quebec, a good Ranger was to "shoot well, and to endure privation and fatigue."[40]

John Butler took his men to Unadilla, where he was in striking distance of the back settlements of New York, Pennsylvania and New Jersey. Butler hoped to join Sir Henry Clinton, Commander-in-Chief of British forces in North America when he advanced up the Hudson River (which he did not). By breaking up the back settlements, Butler hoped to distract and draw of Rebel forces from fighting against Clinton. It was important to destroy the enemy's harvest before their grain filled the magazines of Washington's army. At Unadilla, Butler could also supply his men and the Indians with them at the expense of the enemy.

By mid-May, Joseph Brant and Lieutenant Barent Frey of Butler's Rangers were out harassing and raiding the settlements. They had been ordered to rescue the remaining Mohawks from the reach of the Patriots. Then Brant and Frey raided the settlements with hit and run tactics, destroying property and what they could not carry off. With them they took grain, cattle and recruits for Butler, as well rescued Loyalists families. In the end, Brant and Frey raided over 150 miles of the frontier, killed and captured 294 men in arms and managed to keep the Rebels disorganized.[41]

In late June, Brant got a message from John Butler to meet him a Tioga Point where the Chemung River enters the Susquehanna River. A council of war was held which lasted about nine days. It was decided Brant would continue to raid to north, while Butler with his 110 Rangers and 464 Indians, mostly Senecas and Cayugas under Sayengaraghta would strike Wyoming, Pennsylvania, a strong Rebel settlement that already had sent two companies east to fight the British. The Senecas were especially anxious to hit the settlements here as they had an outstanding grudge against the settlers, believing they were the rightful owners of the scenic valley.

Floating down the Susquehanna on rafts and in canoes, the combined Ranger and Indian forces put up the their flotilla at Three Islands. There they moved overland encamping on a hill overlooking most of the valley on June 30. That night scouts brought in prisoners and scalps. Two Loyalists also arrived in camp and brought news that the Rebel forces in the valley numbered about 800 men scattered out in the various forts. The Indians, seeing that the Rebels had taken shelter in their forts wished to burns the settlements and slaughter the livestock. Butler was against this idea as he wanted to see if the forts would surrender.

The next day, July 1, the first fort fell. Wintermoot's Fort surrendered without a shot after a promise to the garrison that they and their families would be unharmed. The garrison agreed in return "not to bear arms during the present contest." Jenkin's Fort surrendered shortly after on similar terms, only there were no provisions against bearing arms. The main Rebel fort in the valley - Forty Fort - refused to surrendered when summoned.

With his headquarters set up a Wintermoot's Fort, Butler soon learnt the strength of the Rebels from Cornplanter, who with ten warriors had bellied up a hill and counted the Rebel militia drilling in the fort. On July 3, parties sent out to drive in cattle, brought word that the militia was on their way.

Four hundred Patriot militia under the command of Colonel Zebulon Butler, a Continental officer who happened to be on leave in the valley, and Colonel Nathan Dennison who acted as second in command, marched out of the fort at 1 P.M. to attack Butler. Around 4 P.M. when the Patriots were not far off, Jenkin's Fort was torched then shortly afterwards Wintermoot's Fort went up in flames. Butler hoped this would deceive the Rebels into thinking he was retreating. Then Butler set up his ambush "in a fine open wood" running from a marsh to the river. The Rangers took up position on the left flank, while the Indians, lying flat took the right flank touching the swamp. They were commanded by Sayengaraghta and were ordered not to fire until told to. Taking of his hat and tying a handkerchief around his head, Butler took up position with the Rangers.

The Rebels moved past the burning fort, deployed into line and marched to within 200 yards of the Rangers. They let loose a volley, and then two more as the finally advanced to within a 100 yards of the Rangers and Indians, who so far had held their fire. Now with the Rebels only a 100 yards away, the order came to fire. A terrific volley crashed from Butler's force. The Rebel ranks reeled. "Our fire was so close and well directed, that the affair was soon over, not lasting above half an hour," wrote Butler to Colonel Bolton describing the battle.[42]

The Indians moving along the edge of the swamp, flanked the Rebels on their left and were moving to cut off any chance of retreat. The Patriot's left wing was ordered to fall back to a new position, but thinking that part of their force was giving way, the rest of the Rebel militia retreated. The retreat quickly became a rout and the slaughter began. Some of the Rebels decided to make a try for the river. Some escaped, most were shot down or drowned. The rest ran for Forty Fort. According to Colonel Dennison they lost 34 officers and 268 men. John Butler reported 227 scalps were taken along with five prisoners. "The Indians were so exasperated with their loss at Fort Stanwix last year that is was with difficulty I could save the lives of these few," Butler would report later. The Rangers and Indians had 3 killed and 8 wounded.[43]

The following day, Colonel Dennison surrendered Forty Fort and the rest of the settlement. Butler gave them generous terms of surrender. The inhabitants were to lay down their arms and be allowed to return their farms while Butler would try to protect their private property. The forts were to be destroyed and the Continental stores were to be surrendered. The inhabitants upriver called "Torris" were to remain in "peaceable possession of their farms and unmolested in free trade." Finally the people Colonel Dennison surrendered for were "not to take up arms during the present contest."[44]

When the Indians moved into the forts after the surrender, they did plunder people of their private property and 1,000 homes were torched despite Butler promise otherwise. Butler was unable to control the Indians. Later Butler was to report to Bolton that during "the destruction of settlements" no civilians were harmed, but the Indians gave no quarter to those carrying arms.[45] Unfortunately some inhabitants of the valley fled into the wilderness in terror and some of them perished there. A Ranger deserter named Malcolm Boyd was found among the refugees of the valley and was executed on the spot.[46]

Terror spread along the frontier like wildfire when word of the Rebel defeat at Wyoming became generally known. In June General Lachlan McIntosh, Patriot commander at Pittsburgh, was ordered to mass 3,000 men for an advance on Detroit. After Wyoming, Congress ordered McIntosh to abandon his expedition to Detroit and cut his strength to 1,500 men. The rest of the troops were reserved to deal with Butler.[47]

Butler withdrew his force back to the Indian village of Tioga, but there he was hit by a violent attack of fever and ague along with "rheumatism in the head" and he went on to Niagara to try to recover.

Command of the Rangers was temporally given to Captain William Caldwell. Born in Ireland, Caldwell came to Philadelphia in 1773 to visit an uncle. The following year he was involved in the Lord Dunmore's War on the Virginia-Pennsylvania frontier against the Shawnee. In 1775, Caldwell joined with the Pennsylvania forces as they attempted to drive out the Connecticut settlers out of the Wyoming Valley in the much disputed valley. Back in Philadelphia, Caldwell was soon ran into trouble with the Patriots of which his uncle was one and was forced to escape north for safer territory. Heading north Caldwell joined four British officers who had escaped from the Rebels and were eventually led to Fort Niagara by a Loyalist named William Johnson. At Niagara, Caldwell received the rank of Lieutenant in the Indian Department.[48] When the Rangers were formed, Caldwell was promoted to a Captain with his commission being dated December 24, 1777.

Before Butler left for Niagara he ordered Caldwell to take the Rangers to Oquaga, a mostly Oneida village, and tell the Indians they were there to protect the Indian villages close to the Rebel settlements. Caldwell was further instructed to take any offensive moves he thought necessary. "I would have you give orders to every party you send out to burn and destroy everything they possibly can." Butler continued, "If we can prevent the enemy getting in their grain, their general army, already must distressed, must disperse and their country fall an easy prey."[49] Throughout the summer of 1778 scouting and raiding parties of Butler's Rangers, Indians and Indian Department officers covered everywhere from Carleton Island, at the mouth of Lake Ontario, to Pittsburgh.

While Caldwell was in temporarily command, two Rangers from the Susquehanna region asked to go visit their families. Caldwell refused to let them go, but they went anyway. Caldwell sent out a party after them which shot them on sight as John Butler had issued a standing ordering during the earlier advance on the Wyoming Valley that any deserters would be tracked down and shot on the spot. Relatives and friends however, refused to believe these men were deserting and were quite unhappy about the whole incident.

In late August, Walter Butler returned from Quebec to take over command from Caldwell as he was in second in command in the Rangers. With young Butler came Lieutenant John McDonell of the 84th Highland Emigrants. This young Scottish Highlander of roughly the same age as Walter, had come to the Mohawk Valley from Scotland with his 600 members of his clan in 1773 to take up tenant lands offered to them by a distant relative - Sir William Johnson. John McDonell was soon after sent to Montreal to start a career in commerce as an accountant. When the Revolution broke out, John living in Montreal joined the Royal Highland Emigrants - later to be the 84th - obtaining the rank of ensign. John received some acclaim for his arrest of Thomas Walker a Rebel agitator who "preached up Disobedience & Rebellion." With a small party of soldiers, Ensign McDonell arrived at Walker's house in Montreal which he had fortified against an attack. McDonell ordered him to surrender which Walker refused. Tired of talking, McDonell ordered the door broke in and when his men refused to enter, the Highlander snatched up the lantern and started to enter when he was shot in the arm. McDonell had enough. He threatened to burn the house down if Walker didn't surrender immediately. Walker surrendered. After three years service in Canada, McDonell, now with the rank of Lieutenant, met Walter in 1778 and soon asked permission to join the Rangers which was granted on July 31. With the transfer also came and increase in rank to captain.[50]

With Walter Butler in command in the field, Caldwell, along with Joseph Brant with 200 rangers and 160 Indians moved out to destroy German Flats in mid-September. Along the way five Oneidas were captured and were left where they were found with a guard of three Indians to watch them, although the Oneidas promised not to escape. At the head branch of the Unadilla River, the raiders ran into nine Rebel scouts, three of which were killed. One of the scouts reported to Colonel Peter Bellinger, who had sent the patrol out, of the large Ranger and Indian force. Bellinger quickly called for assistance from the local militia commanders to head to German Flats with the men. The inhabitants quickly scooped up what belongings they could and took shelter in the two nearby forts - Fort Herkimer and Fort Dayton. Caldwell and Brant reached German Flats that night, September 16, but a driving rain, postponed an attack until the following morning. Despite the rain which continued to fall, the settlement north of the Mohawk River was hit first. Cattle were driven off and houses, barns full of grain and mills were torched. After an attack on Fort Dayton was beat off, the Rangers and Indians moved to the south side of the river and torched the whole settlement as they drove off the cattle.

"We destroyed all the grain and buildings on the German Flats . . . except the church and Fort Dayton, and drove off a great many cows and oxen, horses and mares. The oxen were all large New England cattle, kept on the flats for the use of the Continental troops, and we took them out of the enclosure at Fort Dayton within pistol-shot of the fort," later reported Caldwell. In the end the raiders burnt 63 houses and 57 barns full of grain, 5 mills and 1 saw mill. Only the two forts, a church and three houses belong to a minister and two Loyalists were left standing. About 100 cattle that were to be sent to Fort Stanwix, 235 horses, 269 sheep and 229 horned cattle were driven with the raiders when they pulled out around noon. "We would in all probability have killed most of the Inhabitants at the German Flats had they not been apprized of our coming by one of the Scouts getting in and warning them of our approach, and perhaps got their Forts," commented Caldwell.[51]

The militia requested by Bellinger and Continentals under Colonel Ichabod Alden from Cherry Valley arrived after Caldwell and Brant had left, and took out after them but to no avail. The five Oneida prisoners on the other hand had more success. While Caldwell and Brant were torching German Flats, the Oneidas escaped and gathered reinforcements of more Oneidas and Tuscaroras and raided the Loyalist settlement of Unadilla and Butternuts. They took prisoners, including two sick Rangers. The Loyalist women and children were left alone, but the prisoners with exception of one who was adopted by an Oneida chief were handed over to the Rebels at Fort Stanwix.[52]

The Patriot forces decided to strike back at the Indians. A force of about 200 men under Colonel Thomas Hartley moved out from northern Pennsylvania on September 21 and destroyed the Indian towns of Sheshecunnunk and Tioga. With word that Walter Butler and 300 Rangers were 12 miles away at Chemung waiting for them, Hartley ordered his men homeward. With them they took prisoners and scalps. On September 29, Hartley's men were attacked by Indians at Wyalusing, but managed to drive them off. Hartley, on October 1, sent a message to the Senecas accusing them of killing women and children, along with burning prisoners and warned them if this continued their country would be destroyed. The Senecas were incensed. At Wyoming no women or children were killed by them and this is what they thought Hartley was referring to. They also had heard other rumours of their alleged savageries at Wyoming against the innocent.

The second Patriot force to march into Indian country was under the command of Lieutenant Colonel William Butler. On October 1, the Rebel force of 267 men moved out from Schoharie for the Susquehanna River. Reaching Unadilla on October 6, the rendezvous point for the Rangers and Indians preparing to hit the Rebel settlements, the Patriots found no enemy forces there. The next day the Patriots forced a Loyalist from Unadilla to serve as a guide. He led them to Oquaga where the enemy force they sought was supposed to be held up. On October 8, the Rebels waded the Susquehanna and moved into the village which they found abandoned. William Butler later reported that Oquaga was the "finest town" he ever saw. It consisted of 40 houses, most of them log, with glass windows, shingles and stone chimneys. The following day the town was torched, except for one house belonging to friendly Oneida. About 2,000 bushels of corn were destroyed and some of the livestock were driven off with the retreating Rebels.

On the way back to Unadilla, the small village of Tuscarora was razed. Unadilla was torched on October 10, except for the Loyalist's guide home. William Butler's forced reached the Schoharie six days later. It had been a successful campaign for the Patriots as Unadilla would no longer serve as a jump off point for Tory and Indian raiders.[53] "I am well convinced," wrote William Butler on his campaign, "that it has sufficiently secured these Frontiers from any further disturbances from the savages at least this winter; and it will be even, hereafter, difficult for them to distress these parts."[54] He could not have been more wrong.

Captain Walter Butler was rejoined by Captain Caldwell and his force returning from German Flats at Chemung. Butler's force was increased by 400 Senecas, anxious to defend their homeland from Hartley's invading force. Colonel Bolton, commandant of Fort Niagara, sent a few volunteers from the 8th regiment to aid Butler. After Hartley had withdrawn to Wyoming, Walter Butler turned his attention north to the New York frontier. He would strike the Rebels at Cherry Valley.

Walter Butler's force increased at Owego on October 22, where he was joined by Brant and his Volunteers (Brant has a small core of white Loyalists serving under him called Brant's Volunteer). Butler's force now consisted of 200 rangers, maybe 50 volunteers from the 8th and 321 Indians. The bulk of the Indians were Senecas, although there were about 30 Mohawks, and a handful of Cayugas, Onondagas, Delawares and Tuscaroras. Except for the Mohawk who were commanded by Brant, Cornplanter probably commanded the other warriors.[55]

This number decreased when a feud erupted between Butler and Brant. Walter Butler disliked Brant and the two began to argue. The white Volunteers serving with Joseph wore a little yellow lace on their hats, which for some reason Walter took offense to. Recruiting for the various Loyalist units was always fierce as recruiters were to only enlist men in certain areas. Walter angered Brant when he announced that only he had the right to recruit men for the Rangers in the area and threatened to send other recruiters to Niagara in irons. Sick of Walter's arrogance and poor treatment of him, Brant almost left had it not been for the Indians urging him to say, telling him that Butler only commanded the white soldiers. They also reassured him he could take any complaints against the young Butler to his superiors at Niagara when the campaign was over. Brant agreed to stay, but his 90 white Volunteers did not. Disgusted by the treatment of their commander by Butler and his warning to them that if they did not join the Rangers they would be treated as rebels, the Volunteers simply left to rejoin Brant in the spring.[56]

Moving up the east side of the Susquehanna River, about 20 miles from Cherry Valley, Brant and Cornplanter in an advance party with about 40 warriors came upon the tracks of nine Rebel scouts from Cherry Valley. They captured the scouts sleeping by a blazing fire. Commanding the scouts was Sargent Adam Hunter, who had been a loyalist imprisoned at Albany when Walter Butler was being held there. He told Butler that an Oneida had warned the 300 Continental and 150 militia garrison stationed there of the raiders approach and that the Colonel and his officers slept in a house 400 yards from the fort. This was all valuable information to Walter Butler.

Fort Alden located at the settlement of Cherry Valley was simply a stockade built around a church. It was under command of Colonel Alden who had ordered the inhabitant to remove their goods which they stored there when he first arrived earlier in the year. On

41

November 6 word reached Alden that large number of the enemy was coming his way. Brigadier General Edward Hand who commanded at Albany was at Cherry Valley on an inspection tour about the time the warning came. Hand advised the inhabitants of Cherry Valley to take their belongs to the fort. After Hand left, Alden refused to allow the inhabitants to bring their belongings inside the fort and reassured them he had scouts out who would warn them when the enemy got closer.

On November 10, Butler's force slogged through snow and mud while been pelted by driving snow toward Cherry Valley. That night, 6 miles from Fort Alden, Butler halted his force on a hill, thick with evergreens and called together the chiefs to discuss their next course of action. Even though the Rebels had been warned of their presence, Walter doubted they knew they were so close and suggested that as soon as the moon rose, the raiders would push on and hit the settlement. One party of men would surround the house of Robert Wells, where Colonel Alden and his officers stayed and capture them, while the bulk of the Rangers and Indians would surprise the fort. Before the raiders moved out, the snow turned to a heavy rain and the attack was called off for the night.

After intolerable wet night, Butler moved his force at daybreak. It had been decided that Captain McDonell "with two subalterns and fifty chosen Rangers, should march with the Body of Indians, with one part surround the house & cut off communication between the fort and inhabitants while the other began the attack upon the Fort," which Walter Butler was to support with the main body of Rangers.[57]

A mile from the fort, while moving through a dense swamp, two Indians fired at two men cutting wood. One of the woodcutters was killed, while the other was wounded. This man now ran for his life with the warriors in pursuit. Meanwhile, the Rangers stopped to examine their wet firelocks. Joseph Brant took a short cut, trying to reach Cherry Valley before the warriors, who were mostly Seneca, did. Brant had Loyalist friends in Cherry Valley, but he was too late.

Warned of the Rangers and Indians presence by a Mr. Hamble who was on horseback and wounded by the Indians, the Continental officers at the Wells house, bolted for the fort. Most didn't make it. Colonel Alden made it out of the house, but was run down and tomahawked and scalped. A few escaped, but most were killed or captured. Little Beard and his warriors then proceeded to massacre the Wells family. Lieutenant Hare of the Rangers attempted to rush to the aid of the Wells and Dunlop family. He saved Reverend Samuel Dunlop and his daughter from the tomahawk. Some accounts credit Little Aaron, a Mohawk, with this rescue. At any rate they survived that bloody day, many did not.

To Butler's chagrin, the Indians hit the settlement killing and plundering indiscriminately instead of strengthening his attack on Fort Alden with the Rangers. For ten minutes, Butler and his Rangers fired on the fort at a distance of about 70 yards, but to little success. Moving to the other side of the fort, the Rangers destroyed an abandoned blockhouse, but had to move back to the original side they attacked to cover the Indian scattered over Cherry Valley from a sally from the garrison. With the houses and barns in flames and columns of smoke pillowing skyward, Butler sent Captain McDonnell with a handful of Rangers into the settlement to save as many people as they could. Brant was doing the same. Captain Butler would later report, that despite his best efforts, he was unable to save the women and children from the fury of the Indians.[58] In the end 30 civilians were killed, mostly women and children, along with 16 soldiers. Seventy people were taken captive.

Butler broke off the attack on the fort around night fall and made his way back a mile from the valley and camped for the night. Butler and Brant then addressed the Indians trying to persuade them to release the prisoners. The prisoners they did manage to get were placed by the campfires and protected by the Rangers.

The next morning, November 12, while the bulk of the Indians were sent off with a herd of cattle, another attack was launched on Cherry Valley. Captain McDonnell and Brant with 60 Rangers and 50 Indians burned everything in the valley, while Captain Butler waited with the rest of his Rangers at the gate hoping the garrison would come out. They didn't and Butler withdrew after gathering another herd of cattle.

Over the next day or two, many captives were sent back to the Rebels. "I could not prevail with the Indians to leave the Women and Children behind," wrote Walter Butler, "tho the second Morning of our March Capt Johnson (to whose Knowledge of the Indians and Address in managing I am much indebted,) and I, got them to permit twelve, who were Loyalists, and whom I had concealed the first Day with the humane Assistance of Mr Joseph Brant & Capt Jacobs of Ochquaga, to return."[59] In reality over 40 prisoners were returned, but Colonel Campbell's wife and four children and James Moore's wife and three daughters were held. They would later be offered for exchange for Mrs. Butler and her children and other Loyalists women and children being held hostage. One of the Moore's girl was later to marry one of the Ranger officers who on the Cherry Valley raid. Many of the other prisoners were taken home by their Indian captors, where they were held until exchanged.[60]

Walter Butler reported shortly afterwards on the reason for the behaviour of his Indian allies:

"The death of the women and children on this occasion may, I believe, be truly ascribed to the rebels having falsely accused the Indians of cruelty at Wyomen. This has much exasperated them, and they are still more incensed at finding that the colonel and those who had then laid down their arms, seen after marching into their country intending to destroy their villages, and they declared that they would be no more accused falsely of fighting the enemy twice, meaning they would in future give no quarter."[61]

A Mohawk war chief named Captain William Johnson spelled out the raid on Cherry Valley very simply to a Rebel officer, when he told them that they and the Senecas were angry over the Rebels destroying Oquaga. In return they wiped out Cherry Valley.[62]

# CHAPTER 5:
## "THE NESTS ARE DESTROYED . . ."
### 1779

By December of 1778, Ranger strength had grown to six companies. That winter they had a new log barracks, built earlier in the fall on the west side of the Niagara River, to move into. It was also about that time they received their uniforms, which was a dark green coatee with dark red facing. Officer's uniform had gold lace besides being of higher quality than the enlisted men's coatees. "Butler's Rangers" was stamped on the pewter button of the coatees. Their small clothes consisted of green waistcoats, white breeches of wool or linen, white stockings, short gaiters and buckled shoes. Prior to this many of the Rangers had worn linen hunting shirts or frocks dyed green, deerskin leggings or overalls and forage caps. Many would still wear this on campaign, or a combination thereof.

A serious problem was still plaguing the Rangers and that was a shortage of weapons. Rangers were expected to bring their own personal firelocks when they joined, but some didn't have any or the ones they had were in bad shape. Colonel Bolton gave John Butler 100 firelocks but admitted "their wasn't a good piece of flint in the place."

Supplying the upper posts like Niagara, Detroit and Michilimackinac had been some what of a burden. At Montreal, 30 to 40 foot long flat bottom bateaus heavily laden with barrels of salted pork, flour, merchandise and Indian trade goods from England began a difficult journey up the St. Lawrence River. The cargo was unloaded from the ships and placed into the flat bottom boats which were rowed, or sailed if the winds were blowing in the right directions,

45

upriver. At the numerous rapids which plagued the St. Lawrence from Montreal to Fort Oswegatchie, crews of the usually 10 to 12 bateaus brigaded together for mutual support, had to get out of their bateaus and wade or struggle along the shore heaving and pulling the boats through the raging rapids. It was difficult, bone weary work, time consuming and expensive.

At the Fort Oswegatchie the supplies were manhandled out of the bateaus and placed into the holds of schooners and other King's vessels for the rest journey upriver and across Lake Ontario. By the summer of 1778, construction began on a strong post on Carleton Island at the mouth of the St. Lawrence River (ten miles southeast of Kingston, Ontario). The post here would replace Fort Oswegatchie for the transhipment of cargo from bateaus onto sailing ships. Prevailing western winds and a strong current had hampered movement of sailing ships at Oswegatchie. From Carleton Island the supplies were taken to Fort Niagara. The cargo if it was destined for Detroit or further west, would be unloaded at the Lower Landing on the east side of the Niagara River. The goods had to be dragged up the 50 foot escarpment by "windlass and large machine on skids." From there the supplies were loaded on carts and pulled by oxen along the portage road, around the falls to Fort Schlosser or "Little Niagara" as it was known by the fur traders. There the supplies were loaded on bateaus to be taken 18 miles up the Niagara River to Fort Erie, where the cargo was transhipped on schooners for the trip across Lake Erie to Detroit.[63]

This supply route was only open for about six months a year as the rest of the year the St. Lawrence River was froze over. To compensate this, enough supplies had to be brought in to last over the winter until the river broke up. Besides the garrison and Rangers to feed and cloth, Loyalists refugees were constantly arriving adding more mouths to be fed, and as the war progressed there were Indians to be feed. Over 7,300 Indians from various tribes, the bulk being women and children had to be supplied over the winter of 1778/79 alone.[64] With Indian raiding parties out, and crops not being cultivated or destroyed as they would be by the Rebels in coming year, the Indians were in desperate need of food.

Cattle and other livestock were taken from the settlements on the Ranger and Indian raids and driven to Fort Niagara or some of the Indian villages for food, but often is was not enough. The

46

commandant of Fort Niagara Lieutenant-Colonel Mason Bolton would report in November of 1778, "I have already bought up above fifty head of cattle from the People who lately came in here . . . but all this is a trifling supply to the two or three thousands of Indians will certainly assemble here in order to receive cloathing, &c."[65]

In October of 1778, Haldimand wrote to Bolton advising that Loyalist refugees could be used to work the soil near the fort to at least supply the post with bread. The rearing of cattle might be possible too he hoped in time. All this would save the government a lot of expense and effort and off set some of the supply burden on the fort by growing some of their own crops. By March of 1779, Bolton wrote back to inform Haldimand that the raising of corn to supply the post would be difficult and "no advantage for some years could result to this Garrison."[66] Also he reminded the Governor, the Iroquois would be unhappy with them cultivating the ground as the treaty of 1764 with them allowed only that only work be done on the land to support the oxen used on the portage road. Even if grain and cattle were raised, it might cause trouble between the garrison and Indians who "would commit frequents depredations" against the crops and livestock. The soil on the west side of the Niagara River which belonged to the Missisaugas was better advised Bolton. After consulting with gentlemen "on the plan of agriculture", Bolton informed the Governor that Loyalist's farmers with a little stock could be "useful to this Post" by the third year, and would be more useful with each passing year.[67]

Haldimand, in writing to Bolton was persistent in June of 1779 of having the land cultivated near Fort Niagara: ". . . if you can find amongst the distressed families three of four who are desirous to settle upon the opposite side of the river, who are good Husbandmen . . . I would have you establish them there affording them whatever assistance you may think necessary, whether by a little  provision or a few Labourers . . ." He also reminded Bolton, "every useless mouth . . . all Prisoners & Idle people from the Frontiers" were to be sent to Montreal.[68]

While hunger continued to plague the Iroquois and troops at Fort Niagara, a threat to the Six Nations homeland and British control of Niagara loomed. On February 27, 1779, George Washington received authorization from Congress  to organize a major offensive against the Iroquois and secure the suffering New York frontier, which was being driven back east and grain and other valuable foodstuff were being destroyed instead of going to the Continental army. Command of the expedition was first offered to Major General Horatio Gates who refused, then the offer went to Major General John Sullivan who accepted.

For months, Washington collected and poured over information on Iroquois country trying to decide the best route to take and determine the amount of supplies and troops required. In a letter to Sullivan on May 31, Washington explained Sullivan's objectives in the grand plan, "The immediate objects are the total destruction and devastation of their settlements. . . . It will be essential to ruin their crops in the ground and prevent their planting more."[69] A total destruction of the Six Nations towns and crops would force them to either make peace or become more of a burden on the already strained British supply line.

Sullivan's force was to consist of 3 brigades and artillery and was to move out from Easton, Pennsylvania to Wyoming, Pennsylvania and then on to the Indian village of Tioga, Pennsylvania. There Sullivan was to be joined by another brigade under the command of General James Clinton which was to come down the Susquehanna River from Lake Otsego, New York and rendezvous with Sullivan. The united force was then to move onto Niagara burning everything in there way. Finally a smaller third force of about 600 men under the command of Colonel Daniel Broadhead, was to strike north from Pittsburgh into Seneca country in northern Pennsylvania and western New York destroying villages and crops in that region.

Sullivan hoped to have his army ready to move out of Easton in May. He would be delayed a month as promised supplies were slow in coming and in some cases did not materialize at all. Work on a road that had to be constructed between Easton and Wyoming proved to be agonizing slow. Sullivan did not get his army in motion for Wyoming until June 18. At Wyoming, progress would not be any faster for Sullivan after he reached there on June 23. He would spent the next five weeks waiting for more troops and supplies.

Meanwhile, Clinton had his brigade concentrated at the head of Otsego Lake. There his troops had constructed a dam to hold back the water. Clinton planned to have dam blown which would enable to float his supply boats down the rushing water over the shallow creek where the Susquehanna River begins and onto Tioga. All Clinton had to do now was for orders to move.

Scouts were sent ouf from Niagara to watch Pittsburgh and the Ohio country as well as Fort Stanwix. A Patriot attack on Detroit was feared in February as Lieutenant-Governor Henry Hamilton of Detroit was captured at Vincennes, Illinois in a failed bid to recapture Illinois. Captain William Caldwell and 50 Rangers were dispatched to reinforce Detroit. Scouts soon brought word to John Butler and Bolton of the massing Patriot forces at Wyoming and Canajoharie. The alarming reports were quickly dispatched onto Sir Frederick Haldimand who refused to believe the Rebels could be assembling such a large army. Detroit was the real target of a Rebel expedition not Iroquois country.

More reports of Rebel activity began to filter in. The Onondaga settlements had been attacked by the Patriots from Fort Stanwix killing 12 and capturing 33 Indians, mostly women. Butler quickly moved his Rangers to Canadasaga at the foot of Seneca Lake, to be in a better position to keep an eye on any Rebel activity. As the Rangers moved through Indian country, Butler found the Iroquois starving. Butler reported on May 19 that many of them were in poor health living off nothing but "roots and greens" they had picked in the forest.[70]

Provisions were scarce at Niagara as well as the fleet of "victuallers" from England had not arrived yet at Quebec. Butler sent out raiding parties to take what food and cattle they could from the Rebel settlements and bring it back for the hungry mouths of the Rangers, warriors and their families. Butler exhorted the Indians to plant corn and had every Ranger that could be spared, given a hoe and put to work helping them. It was not enough. By June, the provisions were consumed and the decreasing supply of powder and lead was being wasted by Indians shooting at little birds, trying to get something to eat.[71]

Raiding parties had some success in obtaining provisions, but they also brought back prisoners and refugees that only added more hungry mouths. In one of these raids, Lieutenant Henry Hare and Sergeant William Newbury were captured by the Patriots, convicted as spies and hung. Scouts and deserters brought news on Sullivan's growing army and it was now clear to the men in the field that a serious invasion was imminent. Haldimand still believed otherwise as

49

he explained in a letter to Bolton at Niagara on July 23: ". . . It is impossible the Rebels can be in such force as represented by the deserter to Major Butler . . . I am convinced Detroit is the object."[72]

Hoping to divert some of Sullivan's troops and take much needed cattle, Butler ordered Captain John McDonell and his company of 50 Rangers, 14 soldiers from the 8th Regiment, along with Cornplanter and 120 Iroquois, to raid the settlements on the west branch of the Susquehanna in Pennsylvania. In May, McDonell had received word from the major of the Royal Highland Emigrants, the unit he was on leave from, that he was to return or he would be superseded. Butler intervened on his behalf writing to his superiors wishing him to stay and commenting, "The Indians are very fond of Captain McDonald [McDonell] & upon being told he was going down the Country have particularly requested that His Excellency would allow him to stay."[73] McDonell would be allowed to stay in Ranger service.

On July 24, after a "fatiguing" march through the mountains, McDonell wrote a letter to Major John Butler from his camp located 20 miles from Fort Wallace or Wallis. McDonell informed Butler, "That the enemy mean to attack the Indian Country from Wioming remains no longer a Doubt." From prisoners McDonell had learned of the Rebel strength which was "said to consist of 8,000 men." McDonell figured it was about half that and probably less. McDonell wrote he would send scouts to Wyoming "to watch the motions of the Rebels."[74]

Three days later McDonell and his men arrived at the settlements and that night surrounded Fort Freeland and waited for first light. The gates of the fort swung open early on the 28th as one of the settlers ventured out to look for his sheep. He had not got far before an Indian named Montour attacked and scalped him. While doing so Montour took a wound in the small of his back. For the next two hours the Rangers and Indians fired on the walls and loop holes of the fort, besieging the small garrison and their families. Finally, McDonell offered the garrison capitulation terms which entailed the garrison laying down their arms and they and "all men bearing arms" to become prisoners and taken to Niagara. The women and children were "not to be strip'd of their cloathing nor molested by the Indians and to be at liberty to move down the country where they please."[75] After short deliberation, the garrison consisting "of one Sergeant & 12

Privates of the Continental Troops and 20 of the Militia, commanded by one of the Commissioners of the County" surrendered.[76] Two of the garrison had been killed.

Two hours after the surrender of Fort Freeland 36 (McDonell reported 70 - 80) Patriot reinforcements under the command of Captains Hawkins Boone and Thomas Kemplin caught McDonell by surprise. McDonell placed the blame for being caught unaware on Indian scouts who took after some horses instead of watching for the enemy. The first Patriot volley caused the Indians to retreat, but they soon rallied and hit Boone and Kemplin's left flank. Meanwhile the Rangers and regulars struck the Rebel's front which routed them. A number of Rebels were killed, including Boone. One Indian was killed and another wounded in this affair.

McDonell released the women and children as agreed in the articles of capitulation as he pulled back for the night. One of the older women was unable to walk, causing her husband to request a horse from McDonell to allow her to travel. The next morning McDonell would send a horse to her allowing her husband to take her to safety. That same morning, McDonell with 100 Rangers and Indians torched 5 forts, which the settlers had fled from and destroyed "about 30 miles of a close settled Country." A hundred and sixteen head of cattle were taken when McDonell and his men moved past Fort Wallace, but when they reached Tioga only 62 where left. A few had been lost, but the rest had been taken by the Indians. The Tuscaroras had captured their own herd of 40 or 50 head.[77]

With McDonell's report, along with word from other scouts, there was now no doubt that the Patriots were planning a major expedition into Iroquois country. On July 31, it began. Sullivan began to move his army toward Tioga which they reached on August 11. A scout returned to Sullivan's camp the following day with word that there were Indians and whites 12 miles upriver at the village of Chemung. Leaving a small force at Tioga, Sullivan with the bulk of his army made a night march for Chemung. About 40 Indians under Rowland Montour skirmished with the Patriots who suffered 20 casualties before they managed to drive the Indians off. The forty some buildings of Chemung were torched and Sullivan returned to Tioga to await the arrival of Clinton.

On August 8, Clinton's dam was blown, gushing water over the shallow parts of the waterways allowing the over 200 supply laden bateaus and boats to reach the Susquehanna River. The troops moved along the shore, torching Indian and Loyalist settlements as they made their way downstream. Thirteen cannons fired a greeting as Clinton's troops arrived at Sullivan's camp on August 22 at Tioga.

The combined Patriot army was one of the largest the frontier had seen in years numbering almost 4,500 men. On August 26, the army of Continentals, militia, riflemen, artillery and a small number of Oneidas marched out of Tioga with Brigadier General Edward Hands' Brigade leading the way, Brigadier Generals William Maxwell and Enoch Poor's brigades were on the left and right with Clinton's brigade in the rear. Nestled in the center of the brigades was the artillery, the Wyoming Militia, packhorses and 700 head of cattle. Riflemen under Major James Parr served as advance scouts and flankers to prevent an ambush. Major John Burrowes, one of the officers with the expedition foreboded about the future of the expedition, when he recorded in his journal that they had only 27 days worth of provisions for the soldiers and only old Indian grass for the their weakening horses with a 120 miles to go deep into Indian country.[78]

At the conjunction of the Susquehanna and Chemung River, a supply depot was established called Fort Sullivan. Here remained 1,200 people, including a 250-man garrison, the wounded and sick, boatmen and camp followers.

At Canadasaga, Butler had collected his Rangers and with nearby Senecas was ready to move out on August 16, to intercept Sullivan. The Senecas however would not move till they had their traditional feast and war dance first. The Rangers, although anxious to be moving, could do nothing but wait for them until the next day. Then they headed out for Chucknut, located a mile from Newtown (Elmira, New York). Here Butler was joined by Brant, Sayengaraghta, Cornplanter and other Indians. Butler had hoped to recruit a 1,000 warriors, but only about 300 showed up. To meet Sullivan's large army, Butler had only about 600 men, with over half being Indian and the rest Rangers and a small contingent from the 8th Regiment.[79]

Knowing he was heavily outnumbered, and with his Rangers and Indian allies in poor health due to living of roots, herbs, and the last 8 days subsisting on corn and a little bit of beef, Butler wanted to retreat and send out parties to harass the Rebels on their march and keep them on constant alarm. Brant agreed with the plan, but the

Delawares had other ideas. This was their land and they were going to prevent the Rebels from destroying their villages. The rest of the Indians agreed with them and Butler had no choice but to comply even it was against his better judgement.

Sending his baggage and sick men to the rear, Butler then moved out with his men to where the Delaware and the other Indians chose to oppose Sullivan near Newtown on the August 27. Butler described the place chosen to fight as "a Ridge of about half mile in length, to the right of which lay a large Plain extending to the River and terminating in a narrow pass near our Encampment, so that having possession of the Heights we would have greatly the advantage should the Enemy direct their march that way; on our left was a steep mountain, and a large creek in Front of a little Distance."[80]

After arriving, Butler's force quickly began constructing log breastworks. Fresh boughs and shrubs were cut and placed in front of the breastworks in an attempt to camouflage it. Captain McDonell with 60 Rangers along with Joseph Brant with his warriors and 30 Volunteers took up position on the right flank behind the log breastworks. Positioned in the center was Captain Walter Butler with the remaining Rangers and the small contingent of the 8th regiment. Major John Butler with the old Seneca chief, Sayengaraghta, took charge of the bulk of the Indians and held the left flank.

From about noon to sunset, the Rangers and Indians waited for the Rebels who failed to appeared. Scouts soon informed Butler that Sullivan had encamped his army near Chemung. With Rebel army bedded down for the night, the Rangers and Indians retreated a mile back to their camp and rested for the night as well. Early the next morning, the Rangers and Indians were back behind their log breastworks waiting, but still no sight of the Rebels.

For a third time, the tired and hungry Rangers and Indians manned their position again on August 29. On the left flank, some of Indians changed their position and turned it along the mountain thereby opening it up for a possible flanking attack. The danger of this move was pointed out to them, but the Indians still refused to budge from their new position.[81]

At about 2 P.M, a party of Patriot riflemen appeared along the edge of the woods. Tall grass on the open plain helped conceal the camouflaged breastwork from the scouts, but these were frontiersmen and sensed something was wrong. One of the rifleman climbed up a tree to have a better look. It was not long before he spotted the breastworks and vermilion painted Indians lying behind it. Any chance the Rangers and Indians had of ambushing the Patriots was now gone.

Messengers quickly ran back to inform Sullivan of their locating the enemy, while the main body of riflemen opened up on the Indians. Hand's brigade held up behind the riflemen and waited for the rest of the brigades to move up. Meanwhile, small group of warriors advanced out of their position to skirmish with the riflemen then retreated back hoping to draw them into a trap. The riflemen were to woods wise to fall for that old ruse.

With the sound of musketry intensifying, Sullivan began to organize his brigades for the coming engagement. While Poor formed his brigade on the right and Clinton's men on the left behind Hand, scouting parties were sent out to scout see if Tories and Indians held a chain of hills to the right of the Patriot's position. Sullivan ordered Poor to try to gain the rear of the Rangers and Indians and hit their left flank. Clinton was ordered to follow Poor and act as a rearguard. Colonel Mathias Ogden's Regiment was ordered along the riverbank on the left to cut off any retreat of the enemy in that area. Hand, with Maxwell's brigade was ordered to attack the enemy's front.

For a mile, Poor and Clinton's men slowly made their way through a thick swamp and then were forced to wade across a wide creek. Ahead of them lay a hill, which they just began to climb up which would put them in a position to hit the adjusted Indian's left flank, when the artillery opened up. This was the signal for the attack, but Poor and Clinton's brigades were not in position yet.

Predicting what the Rebels were up to, Butler and Brant urged the Indians to retreat to a better position. The Indians refused to move until grapeshot and cannon balls smashed into the breastworks and then fall behind them. "The Shells bursting beyond us made the Indians imagine the Enemy had got their Artillery all round us and so Startled and Confounded them that great part of them ran off," reported Butler later.[82] Thinking they were surrounded, some of the warriors fled for the rear, taking the baggage horses and galloping to safety. Outnumbered, the Rangers and remaining Indians continued to fight as best they could but were soon forced to give ground. Carrying their wounded and fighting from tree to tree, the Rangers and warriors fought their way out of the encircling Rebels. After a mile long running fight, the Rangers and Indians scattered only to rendezvous 5 miles at Nanticoke Town just before dark. Major John Butler narrowly escaped capture and it was in the evening before his son, Walter showed up with a little over 40 men and officers, dispelling the fear they had fallen into Rebel hands.

In the fight, the Rangers lost 5 men killed or captured and 3 wounded, while the Indians had lost 14 killed and 9 wounded. The defeat would have serious consequences on the Indians feared John Bulter unless large number of reinforcements were quickly sent in.[83] Butler was right, many of the Indians now only thought of getting their families out of harms way instead of rallying to stop Sullivan.[84]

The Patriots had suffered 3 killed and 39 wounded, some of which would later die from their wounds. The next day after the battle, Sullivan's men began, which they would do many times in the coming months, cutting down corn stalks, some 16 feet high, as well destroying beans, pumpkins and other vegetables. Lieutenant William Barton of the 1st New Jersey, described in his journal of a small party he sent out to find dead Indians. Around noon they found two and skinned them "from their hips down for boot legs: one pair for the major and the other for myself."[85]

Sending his wagons, wounded and artillery back to Fort Sullivan at Tioga, Sullivan 's men, carrying only half allowances, expecting to live off the crops they were going to destroy, marched onto the next principal village, Catherine Town. It was a rugged journey off 14 miles with over half being through a swamp. Many of the packhorses got stuck in the swamp or mud holes while one creek had to be forded 17 times. It was around 11 P.M. when the exhausted soldiers reached the Indian town.[86]

The folowing day, September 2, the town was razed, along with the crops and livestock not used by Sullivan's men. An old Indian woman figured to be 120 years old was found hiding as the town was being torched. Being too weak to follow after her people, the Patriot army built her a shelter and left plenty of food for her before they pushed on.

More towns were set ablaze as Sullivan moved further into Indian country. Kendaida, with its 20 hewn log houses, went up in flames on September 5. The abundant apple and peach orchards at the village were also destroyed. The army then headed north for the Kanadesaga, chief town of the Seneca.

While the Patriots pushed deeper into Iroquois Country, Butler attempted to rally the Indians with little success. Butler hoped to harass Sullivan's army before they reached Kanadesaga, but with half his men sick and with little Indian help, Butler fell back beyond the Genesee River. On September 7, Sullivan reached Kanadesaga which was an impressive place with peach, cherry, apple orchards and large cornfields. The following day the 50 buildings of the town were torched along with the cornfields and orchards.[87]

Sullivan turned west and destroyed the towns of Kanandaigua and Honeoye, and then headed south reaching Great Tree's town. Lieutenant Thomas Boyd with 26 men, was sent on ahead by Sullivan to scout onto Chenussio. Becoming disoriented in the dark, Boyd's scouts reached the abandoned town of Gathsegwareohare. At daybreak, after having dispatched two men with messages to Sullivan, Boyd and his men killed an Indian and wounded another returning to the village. After scalping and mutilating the dead Indian, the scouting party headed back to rejoin Sullivan.

As Sullivan approached the Genesee River, the Indians started to rally. John Butler at Kanawagoras was gathering a force on warriors and Rangers to stop the Rebels before they reached Fort Niagara, which Bolton was very concerned was Sullivan's goal. The Niagara commandant sent the light company of the 8th to reinforce Butler. With roughly 400 Rangers and Indians, plus a Light Company of the 8th regiment, John Butler set up an ambush on September 13 near Kanaghsaws, where the Rebels were constructing a bridge across a swamp at the head of Lake Conesus. Butler's plan was to attack part of the Rebel army as it crossed the bridge and prevent the remainder from assisting them. Taking cover in the dense thickets, the Ranger and their Indian allies listened to the Rebels felling trees as the construction of the bridge came closer.

Lieutenant Boyd and his scouts were returning from their recon when they stumbled unaware into the Rangers and Indian's ambush on September 13. Indian muskets bellowed killing most of the Rebel scouts. Only a handful escaped while Boyd, Michael Parker, and an Oneida serving with them were captured. The Oneida was quickly killed by the Indian and then scalped and mutilated along with the other dead scouts.

After being questioned by Butler, Boyd and Parker were sent under a Ranger guard to Little Beard's Town also called the Genesee

Castle with intention of going on to Fort Niagara. Entering the Indian town the Ranger guards were overpowered by the Indians who took Boyd and Parker and tortured them to death.[88]

With the ambush discovered, Butler had no choice but to fall back to Buffalo Creek as most of the Indians deserted him. Sullivan pushed on reaching the Genesee Castle, a large village consisting of 128 houses with large cornfields nearby on September 14. Here the Patriot army discovered the mutilated bodies of Boyd and Parker who were given a military burial. After the town was destroyed, Sullivan halted his army. With the season growing late, supplies low and satisfied there were no more villages west of the Genesse River, Sullivan ordered his army to turn back. and headed home. The Cayuga villages were yet to be destroyed which was carried out by Lieutenant Colonel William Butler and Colonel Henry Dearborn. Other villages missed were now destroyed on the return journey. Along the way and old Indian women and boy were left a house to live in, but some soldiers locked them in it and torched it.[89]

Reinforcements were on there way to join Butler. Sir John Johnson with the King's Royal Regiment of New York, a detachment from the 34th, the Hanau Chasseurs and a contingent of Canadian Indians were on their way from Carleton Island to help. Caldwell's company of Butler's Rangers were also recalled from Detroit and when they arrived they pursued after Sullivan to Tioga but did not engage the Rebels. Johnson reached Niagara on October 4 after being driven there by a storm instead of landing at Genesee where he planned. At Niagara Johnson was delayed a couple of days by holding a council with the Indians and it would not be until the 10th till he left for Genesee. It was now too late to head for Tioga, so Johnson, along with 200 Rangers under John Butler set sail in 3 vessels for Oswego, while Brant and his men moved overland. At Oswego the plan was to move inland and destroy an Oneida village. The attack never materialized as three Oneidas were captured prowling near Johnson's camp and revealed that the Oneida knew they were coming having been warned by a Cayuga from Niagara. With the element of surprise gone, the attack was called off, with Johnson heading to Montreal and Butler returning to Niagara.[90]

Tioga was reached by Sullivan's army on September 30, and was back Easton fifteen days later. Sullivan had destroyed 40 villages, 160,000 bushels of corn, plus orchards and fields ripe with vegetables. The Iroquois were shaken and had been severely punished, over 5,000 of them sought refuge at Fort Niagara in September alone. With loss of their crops, the Iroquois were now more dependant on the British for their survival. At the same, their grievance against the Rebels grew. The Iroquois were damaged, but they were not broken. Major Jeremiah Frog summed up the situation best when he wrote: "The nests are destroyed, but the birds are still on the wing."[91]

Another attack into Iroquois country, specifically Seneca country set out from Pittsburgh under Colonel Broadhead with 600 men on August 11. Broadhead surprised and defeated a Seneca hunting party at French Creek, Pennsylvania, then moved up the Allegheny River, destroying Delaware and Seneca villages along the way. On the way home more villages were torched with the Patriots finally reaching Pittsburgh on September 14. In their month long campaign, Broadhead's force had destroyed 130 buildings, 500 acres of corn and captured $30,000 worth of fur.[92]

## CHAPTER 6:
## "... THE BIRDS ARE STILL ON THE WING"
## 1780

The winter of 1779-80 was one of the severest in memory. Snow was five feet deep while the Niagara River war froze over from January to March. Starvation haunted the Iroquois as provisions and game was scarce. In the refuge camps around Fort Niagara, 2,600 Indians endured the cold in hunger in their wigwams and shelters. Smallpox, dysentery and yellow fever broke out in the camps killing hundreds as did starvation and exposure. The fort's garrison along with the Rangers and Loyalist refuges also suffered from the lack of food and cold. Dr. James McCauseland, surgeon general of the 8th Regiment, treated scurvy, malnutrition, dysentery and a multitude of other aliments that winter.[93] Scouting parties did not leave Niagara until late February.

In the winter the Rangers were exercised and trained in the use of two field guns, called grasshoppers. They also underwent personal training as described by Governor Haldimand: "Rangers are in general separated, and the nature of their service little requires the forms of parade or those manoeuvers practised in the field. It is the duty, and I am persuaded the pleasure of every captain to perfect his company in dispersing and forming expeditiously, priming and loading carefully, and levelling well. These, with personal activity and alertness, are all the qualities that are effective or can be wished for in a ranger."[94]

Recruiting officers for the Rangers were having success enlisting new recruits. By September of 1779 they were up to six companies. With the new companies, John Butler was promoted to

Lieutenant-Colonel in February of 1780. Captain McDonell was given permission to the stay with the Rangers and was appointed paymaster for the Corps. He and Walter Butler spent the winter in Montreal to settle the Ranger's accounts. Walter wrote of their time in Montreal, "We do very little else but feasting and Dancing, it has nearly turned my head - I find it as hard as Scouting - in order to change the Scene McDonell and me intend to make the Tour of the mountain every other day on Snow Shoes."[95]

By February, the Indians were making snowshoes and war parties were assembling of various sizes. The raiding started earlier against the Rebel frontier and would continue throughout the year. With the coming of spring, the Indians were busy at work planting corn fields. The plan to settle Loyalist farmers on the land west of the Fort, across the Niagara River was again pushed by Haldimand in a letter to Bolton deliver by Lt.-Colonel John Butler:

". . . you will be made acquainted with my intentions of settling Families at Niagara, for the purpose of reclaiming and cultivating Lands to be annexed to the Fort, the expediency of this measure is sufficiently evinced, not only by the injury the service has and must always suffer from a want of a sufficient supply of provisions as well as for the present unavoidable consumption of the Indians, as for the support Troops. . . .

"My letter to Col. Johnson whom I refer to you for the particulars, will inform you of the situation I have chosen at Niagara, which he is directed to purchase from the Mississagues Indians. Lieut.-Colonel Butler with whom I have conversed fully upon this subject has promised to give you every assistance in his Power & from his knowledge of farming . . . ."[96]

To do the actual farming, Haldimand told Butler to take Loyalist farmers he found around Montreal, but Butler as Haldimand continued, ". . . informs me there are some good Farmers in his Corps who either advancing in years or having a Large Family he could dispense with."

The same day, July 13, Haldimand wrote the letter to Bolton he also wrote one to Colonel Guy Johnson telling to purchase ". . . the Tract of Land belonging to the Messessaguas, opposite to the Fort, bounded by the River Niagara, and what is called the four Mile Creek, extending from Lake Ontario to Lake Erie in a Parallel line or near it, with the river, taking the advantage wherever it can be done, of a natural boundary . . ."[97]

Guy Johnson would be unable to conduct a treaty with the Missisaugas in 1780 as they were spread out over their hunting grounds. It would not be till May of 1781 that the land was purchased from the Indians for 300 suits of clothing. Not waiting for the treaty, settling of the Missisauga's land commenced anyway, but it was not to be considered permanent. The farmers were to "hold their possessions from year to year which will be granted to them by the Commander in chief for the time being according to their merits." The farmers were to pay no rent and they were "allowed a reasonable amount of provisions for the space of twelve months after they are put in possession of the Lots." Steel ploughs and "other implements of Husbandry" were to be supplied to them. The produce harvested by the farmers "over and above their own consumption is not to be removed from the Post but disposed of to the commanding officer for the use of the Troops and not to Traders or accidental Travellers."[98]

In early August 1780, the first Loyalists starting working the land having it ready for fall wheat, but it was not planted as the seed arrived too late in the season. John Butler also requested for the families in the following year a forge, which had been promised earlier but never arrived, four grindstones, hoes, dressed leather to make harnesses, along with spring wheat, buck wheat, Indian corn and oats. The farmers would receive them when the supply bateaus arrived in 1781.[99]

Captain McDonell, in June 1780, was ordered to head into Oneida country along the Mohawk River and escort them to Niagara away from the Rebels to join many other Iroquois gathered there. Earlier a pro-British Onondaga chief had threatened the destruction of an Oneida village if they did not go. Help was sought from the Patriots at Fort Stanwix by the Oneidas but it was slow in coming. On June 24, McDonell with a force of 60 Rangers and about 100 Indians arrived at Old Oneida village. A council was held and the Oneida said they did not want to leave complaining of the imprisoning of two Oneida and two Fort Hunter Mohawks who had gone to Niagara to deliver a message for the commander of Fort Stanwix. The following day after the arrival of Spruce Carrier, a Seneca chief, with a war party, a second council was held in which the Oneidas finally conceded to go to Niagara. " . . . they are very sorry for their past behaviour" reported McDonell to the commandant at Fort Niagara, and in the future they would "behave like dutiful children."[100]

Eleven warriors left with McDonell, with the request that their chiefs be allowed to return and see to their families. The journey back to Niagara was terrible for McDonell who was sick with fever and ague. He had to be tied to his horse to make the journey. To make matters worse, provisions were low causing the men to have to eat their horses and dogs. By early July, over 290 Tuscaroras, Onondagas and Oneidas had moved to Niagara.[101]

The ordeal was not over for these people yet. Those who arrived at Niagara were ordered to join war parties going out as a penance for their pro-Rebel activities. Joseph Brant, with over 300 warriors, including some ex-Rebels, burned the abandoned Oneida village of Canowaraghere. The Indians had fled their village for Fort Stanwix, but not all made it. These were overtaken by Brant's men on July 26 and pressured to decide to go to Niagara. Brant then continued on to hit the settlements.[102]

Raiding continued throughout the summer of 1780 by Rangers and Indians along the Pennsylvania and New York frontier. By late August, a massive raid was starting to be planned. Haldimand wrote to Sir John Johnson, was to command the expedition:

"The Treachery of the Onidas and constant obstacles they present to our Scouts in any attempt upon the Mohawk River makes it a matter of serious consideration to compel them to relinquish the Rebel Interest, or to cut them off. The present seems a favorable opportunity for the undertaking, not only to effect that purpose but to destroy the Crop, from the favorable appearance of which the Enemy promise themselves a Large supply and have assembled some force to protect it . . .."[103]

Destruction of the enemy's granaries as events unfolded was to the biggest objective of the raid.

The expedition was to consist of a contingent from Carleton Island and Montreal numbering over 200 men, the bulk from the King's Royal Regiment of New York, but soldiers from Von Kreutzbourg's Hesse Hanau Jaegers and Captain Leake's Independent Company were present as well. Johnson was to take this contingent to Oswego where he would meet a larger contingent coming Niagara. The force from Niagara consisted of 160 men from the 8th, 34th and an artillery detachment manning a Cohorn mortar and a 3 pounder gun called a 'Grasshopper'. Over 260 Iroquois under Brant, Sayengaraghta and Cornplanter, and 156 Rangers from the companies of McDonell, Andrew Thompson and George Dame (Caldwell's company was at Detroit and Walter Butler was sick at Montreal) completed the contingent from Niagara. For John Butler, who was in charge of the Niagara contingent, this was his first field command since the Sullivan campaign. Sickness had plagued Butler since the Wyoming campaign.

Haldimand wrote to Bolton informing him not to "send a man who is not a good marcher and capable of bearing fatigue." Officers were to be selected by the same standard and not by seniority. Despite Haldimand's order for healthy men, "Fluxes, Fevers, and Agues" had weakened the troops at Niagara, forcing Butler to bring some men barely able to carry their muskets.[104]

On September 21, Johnson arrived at Oswego and was joined be John Butler and his Rangers on September 29. Two days later the second vessel, carrying Brant and his men, plus elements from the 8th and 34th, arrived from Niagara after being blown off course by a strong gale. The following day, the Loyalist soldiers, British Regulars and Indian warriors moved out along the Oswego River as 18 bateaus, filled with provisions and artillery were taken upriver to the Three River Junction, then onto the Onondaga River to Lake Onondaga. At the end of the lake the boats were beached at a destroyed Onondaga village on October 5. There the artillery and provisions were unloaded, with some of provisions being concealed for the return journey. Ten days worth of rations were doled out to the soldiers and with the artillery placed on specially built sleds, Johnson moved his force, minus Captain Leake and 15 men too ill to continue on, into Oneida country reaching the village of Old Oneida on October 8.[105]

There they met 15 Indians returning from a scout with four prisoners. The prisoners revealed bad news - the Rebels knew they were coming having been informed by two Oneidas who had gone to Albany with the news that Butler and Brant had left Niagara with 800 men headed for the Mohawk River. The raiders were expected to come down the Sacandaga River as Johnson as did in a raid into the valley in May. Other Rebels were alerted at Canajoharie.

The situation got worse on October 9, when an Oneida deserted Johnson's force carrying with him an empty mortar shell and headed for Fort Stanwix with proof that an enemy's expedition was under way. Rebel prisoners brought in on October 12, this time from German Flats also told of the two Oneidas who had gone onto Albany but they also brought the news that the inhabitants did not know Johnson was so near. This was better news at least.[106]

While Johnson moved inland from Oswego, another raiding force moved south from Lake Champlain under the command of Major Christopher Carleton. The main purpose of the raid was "to draw the attention of the Enemy" from Johnson, but the raiders did destroy a number of houses, barns and mills. They also captured Forts Anne and George. A third party under the command of Captain John Munro attempting to cut their way from Lake Champlain to join Johnson on the Mohawk River were forced to turn back, but not before they destroyed a good part of the town of Ballston and took a number of prisoners.[107]

Johnson's force had almost exhausted their 10 days worth of provisions by October 13. A party was quickly dispatched to "a Scotch settlement", located 20 miles from Schoharie, to get cattle. In the meantime, to combat the immediate hunger, the officers gave up most of their horses to be butchered and ate. Even Sayengaraghta gave his horse up for the dinner plate. About this time 20 Cayugas left to raid of to German Flats and it was with great difficulty the other Indians were prevented from joining them as it was rumoured that a force of 2,000 Rebels were was waiting for Johnson in the Schoharie Valley.[108]

Food arrived on the hoof for the raiders as they continued on toward the valley, when the foraging party sent out to get cattle rejoined Johnson on October 15 with 11 cows. The cows were quickly butchered and devoured.[109] Pushing on Johnson's raiders encamped on October 16 about 3 miles from the "Upper End of the Settlement of Schoharie."

From six captured Rebel scouts that the Senecas had captured earlier, Johnson learned of the strength of the three Rebel's forts in the Schoharie Valley. The three forts that Johnson's men faced in the Schoharie were as follows: the Upper Fort which consisted of picketed walls, with blockhouses in the corners, surrounding a house and barn. The Middle Fort, located near Middleburgh, consisted of a large stone house with a barn and another building acting as barracks. Two blockhouses and a stockade completed the fort. The Lower Fort, consisted mainly of a limestone church surrounded by a stockade and two blockhouses.[110]

In the darkness of the early morning of October 17, Johnson's force moved out, hoping to slip past the Patriot's Upper Fort to hit the Middle Fort. A man looking for his cattle spotted the rear guard of Johnson's force and quickly alerted the garrison of the Upper Fort. Three canons boomed warning the inhabitants that the enemy was in the valley.[111]

With his presence now known, Johnson ordered all buildings, granaries and livestock destroyed, expect those belonging to known Loyalists. A three mile trail of flaming houses, barns and other buildings flickered in the early morning as raiders came upon the Middle Fort. From this fort came 20 men who ventured out to determine the size of the raiding force. The Indians quickly drove them back into the fort and Johnson's arriving men began to surround the fort. After a sortie from the fort was easily repulsed, Butler's Rangers and the Indians began firing at the loopholes of the fort. The 3 pounder and the mortar were soon moved into position and opened up on the fort, but to know avail. The artillerymen handling the guns apparently were not trained well enough in their use for they did little harm to the Patriots, although one mortar shell did crash through the roof of a house setting the beds on fire. This was quickly extinguished.

Deciding the artillery was having little effect, Johnson sent Captain Andrew Thompson of Butler's Rangers with a flag of truce to compel the fort to surrender. Inside the fort confusion reigned. There were about 150 Continentals and 100 militia, plus the civilians who bolted to the fort for protection. Major Melancton Woolsey, commander of the Continentals was interested in hearing what terms Johnson was offering. The other officers in the fort thought differently. Having no intentions of surrendering, border legend Tim Murphy, who was in the fort, aimed his rifle at the advancing Thompson carrying the flag and fired. Fortunately for Thompson, Murphy missed. Woolsey angered at Murphy's action ordered him arrested, but was prevented from doing so by some of Murphy's friends. Johnson ordered his artillery to continue firing, but the fort held.[112]

Deciding he had wasted enough time on the fort, Johnson "ordered the whole to move forward, Killing and destroying everything within fifty yards of their Forts."[113]    Houses, barns, haystacks lay burning and smoldering behind them as Johnson's force moved north toward the Lower Fort reaching it around 4 P.M... Cannon fire greeted the raiders as they came upon the fort, which Johnson, knowing he didn't have much time, as he was confident the Rebels would be gathering a force to attack him, had his men bypass the fort and continue burning as many buildings as they could. While houses and barns were being torched, the 3 pounder was set up and opened up on the limestone church which was part of the fort's defence. Little damage was done and Johnson's raiders pushed another 6 miles and encamped for the night.[114]

The following day, October 18, the raiders trailed along the west side of the Schoharie Creek on a rough "Road being almost impassable for empty waggons."[115] The Cohorn mortar was ordered by Johnson to be slung across a horse, but instead was buried in the swamp by orders of Major James Gray commanding the 1st Battalion of the King's Royal Regiment of New York, when reports came in that the Rebels were close behind them. The 3 pounder was taken along with great difficulty.

When the raiders got close to the Mohawk River, Johnson ordered Joseph Brant and Captain Thompson with 150 Rangers and Indians to cross the Schoharie Creek and destroy the settlements around Fort Hunter. Smaller parties were dispatched to hit distant farms. No resistance was met by Thompson and Brant as they plundered and torched the abandoned Fort Hunter settlement. Afterwards they rejoined Johnson near the banks of the Mohawk River. Johnson sent part of his force across the Mohawk River, then both forces moved west on both sides of the Mohawk River laying waste to the countryside as far as the "Noses", a narrow part of the river, where they stopped for the night.[116]

Two recent deserters from the Patriots that had joined the Loyalists in the spring, deserted again in the night. They made their way to Stone Arabia and informed the commander there, Colonel John Brown, of the weakness of the raiders on the north side of the Mohawk River under Captain Richard Duncan. Brown had earlier received orders from Brigadier General Robert Van Rensselaer, who was mustering a pursuit force, to check Johnson's advance and Van Rensselaer would support him. To Brown's misfortune, Van Rensselaer would not show up on time.

With about 380 men, Brown moved out on the morning of

the October 19, to attack Johnson's divided force. That same foggy morning, much of Johnson's force on the south side of the river had forded to the north side. Brant's Volunteers took the lead, as Johnson's reunited force continued west. They had not gone far when Brant's men bumped into the advance guard of Brown's force which was driven back into the main Patriot force. Johnson's men quickly gained the heights of Stone Arabia where they faced Brown's men who had formed up in the woods behind a stone fence.

Johnson force consisting of elements of the 8th and 34th and McDonell's Ranger company, with Brant's Volunteers in advance moved forward to engage the Rebels. Brown was killed as the fighting began. Then with Brant trying to flank the Rebel's right, Johnson immediately ordered Captain John McDonell and his Rangers to hit the Rebel's left flank. At the same time, Johnson moved forward with the 34th and 8th and attacked the Rebel center. The Patriots quickly gave way and were routed, fleeing for the two forts at Stone Arabia or to the woods.[117]

"Captain McDonell of the Rangers and Captain Brant exerted themselves upon the occasion in a manner that did them honor and contributed greatly to our success," reported Johnson on the engagement.[118] Johnson's force had suffered only 4 killed and 5 wounded including Joseph Brant who was wounded in the foot. The Rebels on the other hand had suffered about 40 killed including Colonel Brown. In Colonel Brown's pocket, papers were discovered from Van Rensselaer revealing that he was in Fort Hunter the day before with 600 militia and 3 field pieces. The raiders had no time to linger.[119]

Johnson's men quickly set to work torching Stone Arabia, but left the two forts alone as they received canon fire from one of them. The raiders then continued west along the river burning everything "up to George Klock's near the Fort Hendrick Ford" while avoiding fortified houses of the Rebels.[120] Near sunset, after cutting through the woods to avoid more fortified houses and gaining access to the high road, the raiders ran into the Patriots who had taken up position behind fences, houses and orchards. This Patriot force, numbering around 1,200 men, under Van Rennselaer who was in pursuit of Johnson's raiders. Sir John immediately sent out a strong detachment to capture the high ground overlooking the road. Then with the remainder of his force, Johnson moved across the road and formed up his men in an open field with the Rangers taking the right flank.[121]

The militia holding the Patriot's left flank were driven back by Johnson's advancing force. The militia fell back to Fort Nelles where it was rallied and reformed. "The Indians who were all on horseback" with Johnson, flogged their mounts in panic across the river when they saw the size of the Rebel force which greatly outnumbered them.[122] The Patriot militia and levies, along with the Oneidas serving with them began to advance through the woods and using the cover of houses and fences opened up on Johnson's men, especially on the left. Brant's Volunteers were forced back as they faced the threat of being flanked. Johnson ordered elements from the 34th and King's Royal Regiment of New York to seize a house and barn and help hold the left flank. Heavy musketry caused confusion in the ranks of the Rebel militia holding the center and their officers attempted to rally them.[123]

Soldiers from the 34th and part of the King's Royal Regiment of New York attempting to capture the house and barn were driven back under heavy Rebel fire. Johnson ordered his 3 pounder to fire a blast of grape shot to precede a volley of musketry. The battle of Klock's Field, as the engagement came to be known, was over. Johnson retreated, while the Rebel militia fell back into disorder.

Darkness now engulfed the battlefield. Fearing the Rebels would be regrouping and more might be coming, Johnson had the 3 pounder spiked and then with the bulk of his men moved a couple miles west and forded the Mohawk River to the south side. Once across the river, they were met by Indians who guided them into the woods. The dead tired raiders pushed on into the woods, but many managed to get separated in the darkness.[124]

One large party under Captain Parke of the 8th that got separated, was heading in the direction of Fort Herkimer and stumbled onto 60 rebel militia heading home on October 20. Parke listening to the reports of his scout and not knowing the Rebel numbers quickly ordered his men back into the woods. Captain McDonell, who was with Parke's had a different idea. With a handful of Rangers and soldiers from the King's Royal Regiment of New York, McDonell charged the Rebel militia, killing 10 of the them, taking two prisoners and routing the others. Not all the Rangers charged however. Lieutenant Peter Ball refused to support McDonell and prevented several of his men from doing so by telling them "it

68

was too dangerous."[125] McDonell suffered no casualties but was two days catching up with the rest of Johnson's retreating force.[126]

On October 23, Johnson and his raiders arrived at an Oneida village where they captured a Rebel who had unsettling news. The prisoner informed his captors that he was a member of a 60 man party sent out from Fort Stanwix to locate and destory Johnson's boats, but he had taken sick and was left behind. (The Patriots knew of the whereabouts of the boats from Loyalist prisoners and deserters one of which was a Ranger - Benjamin Burton.) Johnson' quickly dispatched a party to overtake the Rebels before they destroyed the boats.

The party marched all night and captured the Rebels having breakfast at Ganaghsaraga. Fifty-two of them were captured, while two escaped and the rest killed. From the prisoners it was soon learned that two Oneidas had been ordered on to destroy the boats. Six Rangers quickly mounted up and galloped after the Rebel Indians. The Rangers, fortunately for the raiders, found the boats safe and sound.[127]

Johnson's force reached the boats on October 25 and embarked the same day reaching Owsego the next day. The raiders, according to Johnson, had suffered 9 killed, 2 wounded and 52 missing. Johnson boarded the sloop Caldwell, with 64 prisoners and sailed for Carleton Island. From there he would travel on to Montreal. Accompanying Johnson was Captain McDonell who was going to Montreal and try to recover his health.

Eighteen of the missing men were Rangers under the command of Captain Dame. They were not missing for long as they arrived a few days later at Oswego along with 30 Indians. There they found three boats and provisions and set out for Carleton Island. (Other accounts report that Dame arrived at Carleton Island with only 9 men and around 20 men.) More missing men were eventually brought in by the Indians.[128]

Behind the raider lay a path of destruction in the Mohawk and Schoharie Valleys. Johnson reported that his force had destroyed 13 grist mills, a number of saw mills, 1,000 houses and barns overflowing with 600, 000 bushels of grain. George Washington acknowledged the seriousness of the Tory and Indian raid when he wrote to the President of Congress on November 7: "The destruction of the grain on the western frontier of New York is likely to be attended with most alarming consequences . . . We had prospects of forming a very considerable Magazine of flour in that quarter previous to the late incursion. The settlement of Schoharie alone would have delivered eighty thousand bushels of grain but that fine district in now totally destroyed."[129]

CHAPTER 7
THE DEATH OF WALTER BUTLER
1781


Throughout the winter small parties were sent out from Fort Niagara
to gather intelligence on the Rebels and gather new recruits for two
more Ranger companies John Butler was raising. Lieutenant Andrew
Bradt (later to be commissioned a captain on September 17), a
nephew of John Butler, led one recruiting party into New Jersey
where he recruited 15 men. Spies even ventured into Albany. A
brother of Andrew's, Lieutenant John Bradt with 30 Rangers and 150
Indians under Brant set out on snowshoes through the deep snow for
Fort Stanwix on February 1. They just missed intercepting 50 sleds
bulging with provisions for the fort. They did however capture 16
woodcutters and killed one. By March 17, the Rangers and Indians
were back at Fort Niagara. The deteriorating Fort Stanwix was
abandoned by the Patriots in May as it was doing little to prevent
raids into the Mohawk Valley.[130]

In early June, Indian Department officer Robert Nelles with
40 Rangers and Indians ambushed a Rebel force of rangers and militia
numbering around 40 men near Frankstown, Pennsylvania. The
Rebels suffered 13 killed, 5 wounded and 7 captured while Nelles had
1 killed and 2 wounded.[131]

More skirmishing continued throughout the first half of 1781.
Patriot Colonel Marinus Willet was placed in charge of all troops in
the Mohawk Valley. He placed his headquarters at Canajoharie with
150 Continentals and militia. The Mohawk Valley was hurting and
had a remarkable decrease in its population. It was reported by Willet
that men capable for militia duty had fallen from 2,500 men to under

800. Willet's opinion on the reduction of the population was that one third of them had been killed or captured, while one third had gone over to the enemy, while one third had headed east to hopefully to find a safer area to live. To make matters worse for the Patriots in the Mohawk Valley, little help could be expected from Washington who was having his own trouble. Almost every settlement had been visited by raiding parties at one time or another.[132]

While raiding parties were hitting the settlements, a general court-martial was being held at Fort Niagara. The new commandant Brigadier-General Henry Watson Powell, who replaced Bolton who drowned in the fall of 1780 when the ship he was aboard went down in a violent storm, acted as president of the court-martial of three Rangers - Lieutenant Peter Ball, 2nd Lieutenant Joseph Ferris and Sergeant Freylick. The three Rangers were charged with trying to stir up a mutiny and sedition (in particular for Ball's case in not supporting McDonell in his charge of the Rebels at Fort Herkimer the previous fall) and writing an anonymous letter to Powell accusing Colonel Butler and some of his officers of capital charges and ungentlemanly behavior. Powell and the 14 officers who judged the accused Rangers found Ball not guilty, Ferris was reprimanded and Freylick reduced in the ranks.

There was other trouble in the ranks of the Rangers. Captain Peter Ten Broeck who was captured with Walter Butler in August of 1777, but unlike Butler was not under a sentence of death, was exchanged in 1780 and returned to the Rangers in April 1781. When young Butler made his escape he complained about Ten Broeck's behavior of showing no interest in making an escape preferring to be exchanged instead. Ten Broeck was commissioned a Ranger Captain on May 4, 1778, while in Rebel custody, but had been removed from the pay list the same day. A court-martial was held in December of 1781 to determine why Ten Broeck had not made an escape attempt even after a Ranger officer was sent to help him. The court-martial cleared Ten Broeck's behavior stating that he had acted proper and had no favorable opportunities to escape. Ten Broeck was angered however when he discovered that Captain McDonell was to be senior to him, even though Ten Broeck's commission dates earlier. Ten Broeck's three years of captivity was deciding factor in McDonell's favor.

Another Ranger officer caused some resentment in the ranks

72

in 1781. Captain John McKinnon was commissioned January 1, 1781 by Haldimand and given the 8th Ranger company. McKinnon, having seen service under Sir William Howe, had been recommended for a position in Canada. Haldimand sent him to the Rangers which not well received by John Butler or some of his officers who put their misgivings in writing. MacKinnon was not to last long in the Rangers as sickness would force him to return to England to try and recover his health.[133] Captain William Caldwell, in July, commanded a large party that was heading toward Schenectady. The plan was to rendezvous with another party moving south from Crown Point, but instead Caldwell overtook a band of warriors commanded by Lieutenant John Hare on August 3. The two raiding parties combined bringing their strength to 87 Rangers and 250 Indians. With provisions running low, the Indian held a council and decided without consulting Caldwell that they would hit a settlement in Ulster County. Not long on their journey toward Ulster County, Caldwell's force came upon tracks, which the Ranger Captain took to be those of a Ranger recruiting party. To be on the safe side, Lieutenant Nelles scouted ahead with a handful of men and soon came upon a party of Rebels. In the ensuing skirmish Nelles scattered the Rebels and took two prisoners.

Forty miles from Caldwell's force was a Rebel fort at Lackawaxen that commanded a narrow pass in the hills the raiders would have to pass through. Caldwell would have preferred to attack it, but the Indians did not want to fearing it would warn the country they were going to hit. The Indians did agree however, to attack the fort on the return journey. The Rangers and Indians slipped past the fort under the cover of darkness. Another fort at Neversink was bypassed the same way on August 11. Then they struck the settlements that lay before them. Two mills were destroyed along with 30 houses, plus a large quantity of grain. A large number of horses and cattle were captured. Caldwell sent some of his Rangers to destroy Nipenack and Monbackers when the Indians refused to budge being heavily overladen with plunder.

Caldwell's force was deep in Rebel territory as 12 miles away lay Kingston, near the Hudson River. The militia of Ulster County quickly began to assemble, with two Regiments on the move toward the raiders from different directions. Undisturbed by the advancing Rebels, Caldwell slowly withdrew into the woods driving the cattle with them hoping to lure the militia after him. The Rebels let him go, but not all was well as Caldwell reported to Colonel Butler, "On our return we had the mortification to see the Indians kill and take the greatest part of the cattle captured by the rangers, which would have left us in a starving condition were it not for the horses we had taken."[134]

In early September, a force of 74 Rangers and Indians under Lieutenant John Clements of the Indian Department, headed toward German Flats were they were spotted by the garrison. The Patriots sent out about 40 men from the fort at German Flats to scout for the enemy. The Rangers and Indians knowing of their advance set up an ambush and sprang it on the Rebels with a bloody volley. They then rushed upon the Rebels with their tomahawks killing 21 men and capturing 8.[135]

While raids were being carried out in the Mohawk Valley and Ulster County, the Rangers were also active in the west fighting out of Detroit where a company was stationed. The year before, 1780, had seen the Rangers helping to bolster the morale of the Shawnee who's villages along the Ohio River had been destroyed. New recruits were found for the Rangers from prisoners taking in a campaign led by Captain Henry Bird against some of the forts in Kentucky. Almost 400 prisoners were taken when Ruddle's Station and Martin's Station surrendered to Bird in June of 1780. Haldimand wrote that many of these prisoners (a large number being German) be allowed to farm near Detroit, Niagara and Carleton Island. Twenty of them chose to serve in the Rangers.[136]

Captain Thompson moved his Ranger company deep into Indian territory when a Rebel force under the command of Colonel Daniel Brodhead crossed the Ohio River and destroyed the Delaware village of Coshocton. Brigadier General George Rogers Clark, the great Patriot commander in the west, had long being eyeing Detroit. The British were aware of his intentions and had been attempting to thwart it. Thompson's men ended up being stationed at Sandusky for two months, waiting to see what Clark was up to.[137]

By the middle of August, Clark began assembling 400 men at Wheeling for an attempt on Detroit. Over a 100 men under the command of Colonel Archibald Lochry were to join Clark, but as they were late in arriving, Clark pushed off down the Ohio River.

Desertion was plaguing Clark's little army and he met to get them as far away from their homes as he could. Lochry was ordered to catch up.

Thompson and his company of Rangers, along with a number of warriors under the command of George Girty, Alexander McKee and Joseph Brant who had been sent to Detroit in April, quickly moved to intercept Clark. Brant and Girty moved on ahead and took up position at the mouth of the Great Miami River where it joins the Ohio River. Brant could do little on the night of August 18-19 when Clark passed by. The Rebels were too strong, but three days later Brant did intercept a boat carrying supplies for Lochry. From these prisoners, Brant and Girty learned that Lochry would be passing by in a few days. An ambush was set up.

Eleven miles below the Great Miami, Brant and Girty watched as Lochry's flotilla came into view on August 24. The flotilla was ambushed with not one Rebel escaping. Lochry with of his 6 officers and 30 men were killed, while the rest were taken prisoner. Five days later Thompson and his Ranger company, with the rest of the Indian force arrived. Simon Girty, brother to George, was also with them.[138]

Brant, Thompson, McKee and the Girty brothers, proceeded after Clark down the Ohio River. On September 5, after reaching the mouth of the Kentucky River, the Rangers and Indians held up to determine whether to attack Clark, who was positioned at Louisville on the falls of the Ohio River. Two Rebel prisoners were brought in four days later with the news that Clark was going to abandon any attempt against Detroit this season. Hearing this and satisfied with their defeat over Lochry, many of the Indians decided to pack up and return to their villages.

The Rangers who had been out of provisions for four days, retreated as well hoping to get food at the Indian villages. Tired and half starved, the Rangers did manage to shoot a bear or two. They also got green corn which they lived on as they stumbled back into Detroit. McKee and Brant were not satisfied to turn back yet. They crossed the Ohio and raided into Kentucky.[139]

In September Haldimand, ordered another big raid into the Mohawk Valley. Leading the expedition, was the "active and zealous" Major John Ross, former captain in the 34th, but recently promoted to a major in the 2nd Battalion of the King's Royal Regiment of New

York and commander of the garrison at Carleton Island since November of 1780. Taking his contingent, consisting of 150 men from the 2nd Battalion of the Kings Royal Regiment of New York, 75 soldiers of the 34th led by Captain Ancrum and 48 men of Captain Leake's company, Ross headed out by water for Oswego, where he was to rendezvous with a contingent from Fort Niagara.

The force from Niagara arrived at Oswego on October 9 after battling a violent gale on Lake Ontario. It consisted of 159 Rangers, with 8 officers under the command of Captain Walter Butler, 36 soldiers from the 8th under Lieutenant Coote and 109 Indians under Captain Gilbert Tice. Ross referred to these Indians as "the refuse of different Tribes without a leading man amongst them" and they were to give him more than one headache before the expedition was over. Ross, who had been waiting at Oswego for a week, ordered an advance the following day.[140]

On October 15, Ross left his boats and provisions under a small guard in a creek flowing into Lake Oneida and headed out for Otsego Lake. Sending out a small party to bring in prisoners, Ross and his men endured terrible weather, as they moved through Cherry Valley and on toward Corrystown. The news from the prisoners was no better than the weather. The Rebels were aware of their presence and the number of militia and Continentals far outnumbered Ross's force. Still, "I was nevertheless determined to render the Expedition as useful as possible," wrote Ross in his report. Ross decided to strike Warrensbush, although it would be risky as it was "lying centrically between Fort Hunter, Schohary and Schenectady."[141]

Ross arrived at Corrystown on October 24, where the alarm guns boomed to warn of his approach. Expresses were quickly dispatched out to warn the other posts and to mobilize troops to intercept the raiding force. Ross would have to move quickly now and he ordered a forced march.

For 14 miles, through a heavy rain, the Rangers, regulars and Indians stumbled along terrible roads for Warrensbush. The troops struggled to stay together, but some were to bone tired to keep up and were left behind. Just before morning, they arrived near Warrensbush and there they rested, weapons ready, until daylight.

When the sun appeared, the Indians and some Rangers were ordered out to destroy the settlement. Ross reported that before noon "the whole Settlement for seven miles was in flames, near one hundred farms, three Mills and a large Granary for Public service were reduced to Ashes, the Cattle and Stock of all kinds were likewise destroyed." The Patriots on the other hand reported only 22 frame and log barns, 1 gristmill and 5,411 bushes of grain were destroyed. With the damage done, Ross and his men knew it was no time to linger.[142]

With numerous Rebel troops bearing down on him, Ross turned and headed for Johnstown. There he crossed the swollen Mohawk River after brushing aside a small party of militia which came out from the fort to reconnoiter the raiders. Ross's intention were to strike for German Flats and follow the trail that led north to Carleton Island, instead of retreating back to his boats, which he feared the Rebels might have captured. There was also the possibility the Rebels, with control of the river, could get in front of him and block his retreat.

Outside of Johnstown the raiders held up. They needed provisions for the long journey ahead. Cattle and horses were quickly butchered up for food. In the late afternoon, Ross just headed into the woods, when scouts brought news that the Rebels were just behind him. Knowing his men were too tired to outrun the enemy without leaving numerous stragglers, Ross decided to fight. A quarter of a mile into the woods, Ross positioned his men and sent out the Rangers as a screening force.

Colonel Willet, in charge of the Patriots, had quickly taken after Ross from Canajoharie, when the alarm was given of his presence. Finally catching up with the raiders after a vigorous night march, Willet sent part of his force to try to attack the rear and flank of Ross, while he prepared to attack Ross head on. His advance guard were driven out of the woods by a volley and an Indian yell from the Rangers. Willet, with his main force quickly moved in and traded volleys with Ross's troops. As the battle raged, the Rebels right wing started to waver. Ross ordered a charge, causing the Patriot's right wing to break. Some of Rebels kept up a running fight to the edge of the woods, where they broke as well. "It was then I lamented the want of a good Body of Indians, (few of those present venturing to engage), in which had I been so fortunate, it would in all probability have crushed the Spirit of the Rebellion on the Mohawk River . . ." or so reported Ross.[143]

The battle was not over yet. The Patriot's left wing was still standing and they held a field piece which bellowed away at Ross.

The raiders charged this position, driving away the Rebels and capturing the field piece - a brass 3 pounder, with its ammo. Still another Rebel force attacked Ross's right, but "seemed rather inclinable to harass than attack openly."[144] This force took cover along the edge of the woods and kept up a "scattering fire". Ross reported how his men, with the support of the captured 3 pounder, dispersed this Rebel force and how only darkness saved the Rebels from "total destruction". Differing in opinion from his commanding officer, Indian Department officer, Captain Tice described the battle "as very obstinate on both sides, which lasted till dark, when we left the field . . .."[145]

In the battle or more accurately set of skirmishes, Ross lost about 20 men killed and wounded. More would be lost straying away because of darkness and utter exhaustion. The Patriot's casualties were similar to the British. In one spot alone, Ross commented on seeing 20 enemy soldiers laying dead.

Ross and his men retreated deeper into the woods and rested for the night. As they continued their retreat the next day, the weather turned foul, pelting them with snow and sleet. It was with great difficulty that they found the trail that led from German Flats to Carleton Island on October 29. The Indians decided they wanted to head back to Niagara and were directing the course of retreat accordingly. With snow falling, Ross called a halt for the day.

Ross thanked the Indians for their good behavior and shook their hands. He was however, disgusted with them for he would later report of the Indians decision to change the escape route "without any regard to our security."[146] When the raiders pulled out the next morning, most of the Indians lingered around camp, preparing to head west, while Ross headed north.

They had not gone far, when the tenacious Willet, who had rallied his force and continued in pursuit, attack Ross's camp. The Indians who still hung around, scattered in the woods just in time to avoid capture. An Indian Department officer, and three officer's servants were not so lucky, as they were captured.

Some of the Patriots caught up with Ross's rear guard and fired at an Indian accompanying the retreat north. Now alerted the enemy was close at hand, Ross and his men quickly moved forward, crossing Canada Creek about 2 P.M.. Captain Walter Butler was left behind with a handful of Rangers to slow down the Rebels. Ross and the rest of the troops moved out in Indian file at a trot to find a place to make a last stand.

The Patriots appeared on the other side of the creek and a short fire fight broke out in the fog that shrouded the area. The fog parted long enough for an Oneida warrior, fighting with the Patriots, to put a ball into Walter Butler. Accounts vary how he was killed. Some say he was only wounded and the Oneida tomahawked him, others say he took the ball in the head and was killed instantly. At any rate he was dead, his scalp lifted and his Captain's commission was taken, eventually ending up in Willet's private papers.[147]

"Although they had been four days in the wilderness with only a half a pound of horseflesh a day per man, yet they ran in their famished condition thirty miles before they stopped," Willet would say later of the raiders, who he decided not to pursue any longer.[148] While Willet was heading home, Ross waited an hour with his men drawn up for battle, then retired as well when no enemy appeared. The seven day march back to Carleton Island was rugged and fatiguing. The jaded men, with little food and some without blankets or overcoats, struggled across swollen streams on rafts and suffered terribly from the weather. They finally reached Carleton Island on November 6.

The raid had cost the British, Loyalist, and Indians 74 men, many who were reported missing. Thirteen of these missing men were Rangers, who eventually made their way to Oswego and safety. The news of the death of Walter Butler was greatly rejoiced over in the Mohawk Valley - more so than the news of the surrender of the British at Yorktown, which reached the valley about the same time.

# CHAPTER 8
## KENTUCKY HO!
### 1782

In April of 1782, almost 185 Rangers commanded by 7 officers accompanied 28 men of the 8th Regiment in going to Oswego. There they joined Major Ross, who arrived from Carleton Island with a large detachment to reestablish Oswego. It was feared the Rebels might make an attempt to establish a post here as it was thought they were planning another invasion of Canada.[149]

The dispute between the seniority of McDonell and Ten Broeck continued into 1782. Colonel Butler wrote to Haldimand's military secretary on June 1 that he wished to have an error corrected in the dates of McDonell's and Ten Broeck's commissions. " . . . it was never my intentions that Captain Tinbrook should take Rank of McDonell, which will appear by the Muster Rolls . . . ." Butler wanted McDonell to be the senior Captain after the death of Walter Butler. Colonel Butler wrote, "Capt. McDonell is the most capable officer in the Corps to command in my absence, which will often be the case if I am to have the care of the Indian Department, he is also the best liked by the Indians . . . ." In November, Butler was informed that McDonell's commission was to predate Ten Broeck's.[150]

Most of the fighting for the Rangers in 1782 was in the Upper Ohio country and Kentucky. Caldwell took command of the Rangers serving out of Detroit. He replaced Thompson who drowned returning to Fort Niagara the previous year.

In March, over a 160 Patriot frontiersmen from Washington County, western Pennsylvania, commanded by Colonel David Williamson, saddled their horses and intended to cross the Ohio and burn the towns of the Christian Delaware. The frontiersmen were sure these towns were being used by the Indians as a jump of points for raids into western Pennsylvania and Virginia. Only 100 frontiersmen forded their mounts across the Ohio River, as the other could not get their horses across and had to turn back. The frontiersmen continued and on March 7 surprised the Moravian Indians at Gnadenhutten. The Indians who had been converted to Christianity by Moravian missionaries made no attempt at escape. Ninety men, women and children were forced into their chapel until the frontiersmen decided what to do with them. A few argued the Indians were Christian and should be taken to Pittsburgh, while others stating articles had been found in the village that had come from raided white settlements and they should be killed. It was the latter argument that won out. The following morning, after a night of prayer, the Indians were brought out and killed by a cooper's mallet.[151]

The success of the raid, inspired a bigger raid that would drive deeper into Indian territory. Over 480 men under the command of Colonel William Crawford headed out on May 25 from Mingo Bottoms along the Ohio River for the Delaware and Wyandot Indians at Sandusky. Their movement was quickly detected by the Indians and assistance was sent by the commander at Detroit, Major Arent De Peyster.

Captain Caldwell and his company, along with some "Lake Indians" sailed of out of Detroit for the Sandusky River to aid the threatened Indians at Sandusky. When Caldwell reached Sandusky he was reinforced by 24 more Rangers under the command of Lieutenant John Turney who arrived from Niagara. Caldwell now had about 74 Rangers and 44 Lake Indians, along with around 150 Wyandots and Delaware commanded by Captain Matthew Elliot of the Indian Department. Simon and George Girty were also present.[152]

Scouts informed Caldwell around noon on June 4, that the Rebels were only a few miles away. The Ranger Captain quickly moved his Rangers and warriors out to meet the Rebels. Crawford formed his men in a grove of trees surrounded by open ground and prepared to fight. Caldwell managed to capture a hold on the woods and slowly drove the Patriots back, allowing most of his Rangers and Indians to have cover. The skirmishing was intense, with war cries piercing the roar of musketry and the crack of rifles. Caldwell was wounded when a musket ball passed through both of thighs.

Command fell on Lieutenant Turney. Darkness finally broke of the fighting.

Both sides encamped where they were for night and with daylight the following morning, the fighting continued, but consisted mainly of long range firing. Around noon, Turney was reinforced when Alexander Mckee showed up with 140 Shawnee. Turney was now able to surround the Rebel frontiersmen, who continued to fight throughout the rest of the day. A council was held by the surrounded Patriots that night and they decided to attempt to breakthrough the enemy lines and escape.

The Ranger and Indian lines were pierced by escaping Rebels in the darkness who were forced to leave their wounded behind. The Indians by daylight were soon in pursuit and hunted down any stragglers. Crawford was captured and was soon to face a horrible death. In revenge for the Moravian massacre Crawford was tortured and burnt to death. When De Peyster heard of torture of Crawford he was disgusted and wrote to Mckee threatening to withdraw the Rangers if such cruelties persisted.

In the engagement the Rangers had 1 killed and 2 wounded besides Caldwell. The Indians had suffered 4 killed, besides an Indian Department interpreter and 8 wounded. The Patriots losses vary depending on whose reporting. Turney said he counted 100 dead on the field, while McKee and Elliot reported possibly as many 250 Rebels were killed. The Patriots give their casualties between 30 and 50.[153]

By July, Caldwell was back in command and was moving his Rangers and about 300 Indians from the Indian village of Wapatomica on the Upper Sandusky toward Wheeling, located on the Upper Ohio, with intentions of destroying Fort Henry there. The Rangers and Indians had reached the Scioto River when an Indian runner from Wapatomica caught up with them and warned that George Rogers Clark was approaching with a large force and artillery. Caldwell quickly pulled back to Wapatomica and then decided to move to the Shawnee village of Piqua, and meet Clark there. McKee in overall command of the Indians, with Elliot and the Girtys had assembled around 1,100 warriors from the Shawnee, Delaware, Mingos, Ottawas and Chippewas.[154]

When no attack from Clark materialized, many of the Indians began to head home. ". . . notwithstanding all our endeavors to keep them together, occasioned them to disperse, in disgust with each other," later reported McKee.[155] With the bulk of the Indians heading home, McKee, Elliot and the Girtys with 300 warriors mostly Wyandots and Lake Indians, with a few Shawnee, Mingos and Delawares, along with Caldwell and 30 Rangers moved onto the Ohio River.

On August 15, Caldwell and McKee crossed the Ohio River into Kentucky and moved onto Bryan's Station surrounding it early the next morning. The fort consisted of 40 cabins with a 12 foot high stockade between the buildings and blockhouses at the corners. Forty-four men were in the fort with their families when Caldwell and McKee appeared. After the Rangers and Indians were detected, two mounted messengers galloped out of the fort and through the enemy lines riding for help.

With torches in their hands the fort was attacked by the Rangers and Indians, but was driven back by the rifle and musket fire from the defenders. Some of the cabins were reached by the Indians and there outside walls were set on fire but an east wind prevented the fire from spreading. Shooting continued through the day between the defenders and attackers with few casualties being suffered by either side.

By the morning of August 17, Caldwell ordered a retreat. His force had managed to burn five cabins, kill over 300 of the fort's pigs, 150 cattle and a number of sheep. They also destroyed a large quantity of the fort's crops and took a number of their horses all that loss of 5 Indian killed and 2 wounded.[156]

The following day, a Patriot relief force arrived at Bryant's Station. When they reached the fort a consul was held to determine what to do next. Some of the Rebel leaders were for pursuing the Rangers and Indians, while a few others wanted to wait for reinforcements under Colonel Benjamin Logan who had about 400 or 500 men and was not far away. After a heated debate it was decided they had enough mean to deal with Caldwell. On August 18, 182 men commanded by Colonels John Todd and Stephen Trigg headed out of Bryant's Station and took after the raiders.

Caldwell with 200 Indians and his Rangers who had been retreating up a buffalo trace had encamped the first night at the ruins of Ruddle's Station. The following day they moved onto Blue Licks where Indian scouts watching the back trail, reported to Caldwell the

Rebels were in pursuit. Caldwell quickly set up an ambush near the ford of the Licking River.

Lieutenant-Colonel Daniel Boone, who was with the Patriots in pursuit of Caldwell along with his son Israel, was uneasy. The Rangers and Indians were doing little to conceal their trail. Boone advised caution, when the Kentuckians reached the ford of the Licking River on August 19. Two scouts who had crossed the ford returned reporting they had seen no Indians. Boone still insisted there was going to be an ambush here.

While the leaders of the Kentuckians determined what to do next, the men moved across the river on their own. They were 60 yards from where Caldwell's force lay concealed when a deadly volley ripped into the Kentuckians. Within three minutes 40 Kentuckians were dead or wounded. The Indians quickly began to work around the Rebel's right. Trigg went down and the Kentuckians under his command began to fall back on the right. The center commanded by Todd was falling back as well. The men with Boone who were on the Rebel's left were having more success, but only briefly. Five minutes into the battle most of the Kentuckians were running for their lives with tomahawk wielding warriors in hot pursuit. Boone, trying to keep his men together, cut west and managed to escape but not before his son Israel was killed.

The Kentuckians had suffered well over 70 casualties, while the Indians had 10 killed and 14 wounded. One interpreter from the Indian Department was killed as well. After the battle, Caldwell continued his retreat across the Ohio River.[157]

While Captain Andrew Bradt arrived at Sandusky with his Ranger company too late to join Caldwell, he moved on toward Wheeling with 238 Indians. He reached Wheeling on September 11 and for three days besieged Fort Henry. Attempts were made on the fort, but none were successful. After the Rangers and Indians had razed everything they could outside the fort, Bradt ordered a retreat.

Bradt joined up with Caldwell and remained a month in Indian country before the tired and half-starved Rangers retired to Detroit. The fighting was over for the Rangers.[158]

# CHAPTER 9
## "THEY WOULD RATHER GO TO JAPAN"
### 1783 - 1784

Official peace came in 1783 with the Treaty of Paris and with it came trouble. Haldimand and the western post commanders were fearful of what the Indians might do once they found out how much of their territory the British ceded to the Patriots in the peace negotiations. The boundary of the American territory, according to the peace treaty stretched as far north as the middle of the St. Lawrence River as well as the middle of the Great Lakes. The Indians were not mentioned at all in the treaty. Although the post commanders tried to keep the conditions of the treaty as quiet as possible, they knew the Indians would find out soon or later. Fearing the Indians might turn on the western garrisons such as Fort Niagara, Haldimand ordered Sir John Johnson, now Superintendent-General and Inspector-General of Indian Affairs in the Northern District of North America, to go to Fort Niagara "to quiet the apprehensions of the Indians until some arrangement can be fixed upon their future settlement."[159]

Johnson had eased the Six Nations fears in the fall of 1782 when there were just rumours of peace, but now they were not just rumors anymore. In the last week of July 1783, Johnson spoke with over 1,600 Iroquois and explained to them their land was still theirs and the King was still their friend. A large amount of presents were handed out to the Indians just to reassure of them of this fact. Johnson urged the Iroquois to hand over any prisoners they might have and cease hostilities against the Rebel frontier.

In the coming years the Iroquois would lose a lot of their lands to the Americans as they would eventually be forced onto reservations. In May of 1784, John Butler, acting on orders from Haldimand, purchased land from the Missisaugas along the Grand River north of Lake Erie as requested by Brant and offered it to any of the Six Nations who wanted to relocate there. By 1785 over 1,800 Iroquois had moved from their homes in New York to the Grand River. Not all the Iroquois chose to move the Grand River. Some settled in a tract of land set aside for them along the Bay of Quinte.[160]

As part of the peace treaty, Fort Niagara was to be handed over to the Patriots, but the British were not quick to give up this fort or their other western posts for that matter. To preserve the alliance of the Indians, check the American westward and northward expansion and protect the infant settlements in what would be come Upper Canada, the British decided to retain these crucial western posts. They would finally turn them over to the Americans in 1796.

In June of 1784 Butler's Rangers were disbanded. There was no going back home for the Rangers. "They would rather go to Japan," John Butler told the commandant at Fort Niagara General Allan Maclean, "than go among the Americans, where they could never live in peace." The Rangers and their families would have no choice but to put down roots some place else and start again.[161]

Land for the ex-Rangers and their families, along with other disbanded Loyalists units who had served in the Northern Department was purchased from the Indians, surveyed and set aside for them along the north shore of the St. Lawrence River, Bay of Quinte area, the Niagara Region. Most of the ex-Rangers moved out of their barracks and settled in the Niagara region. The bulk of the ex-Rangers and their families now had to start over again. Taking up their land grant for service to the King, the ex-Rangers and other Loyalists soldiers had to start clearing the forest to be able to built a cabin, plant a crop and in time form a new British North American colony - Upper Canada and in a few generations a new country - Canada.

Some ex-Rangers, such as Captain William Caldwell chose to head west and settle on the east side of the Detroit River. Caldwell, Matthew Elliot and a few others negotiated land from the Indians there, which was confirmed by Haldimand. Caldwell eventually acquired a fair amount of land in this area and went on to become involved unsuccessfully in commerce. During the War of 1812, Caldwell formed a unit called the Western Rangers and in 1814 became superintendent of Indians in the Western District. Caldwell died in 1822.

Still a handful other Rangers, such as Captain John McDonell, moved east and took up lands along the St. Lawrence River. John McDonell became involved in Upper Canada politics eventually being selected as the first speaker of the house of the colony's first parliament in 1792. McDonell also continued his military career by be given command of the 2nd Battalion of the Royal Canadian Royal Volunteers. After taking command he was soon promoted to the rank of Lieutenant-Colonel. McDonell died in 1809.

Colonel John Butler continued to live in Niagara region and serve in Indian Department as deputy superintendent. Butler had lost his estates during the war and the Loyalists Claims Commissions set up by the British after the war to possibly reimburse the Loyalists for their losses during the war if they had proof, refused a lot of Butler's claims. In the early part of the war, Butler along with a merchant named Richard Pollard, had a monopoly on the Indian Department trade until 1779 when Guy Johnson took control of the trade. After the war, Butler attempted ventures to regain some of his money, most of which were unsuccessful. He was however appointed a justice of the Court of Common Pleas and Colonel of the Lincoln County militia. John Butler died in 1796.

# APPENDIX 1

## THE RANGER CAPTAINS

1    Captain Walter Butler - commissioned Dec. 20, 1777 - killed 1781

2    Captain William Caldwell - commissioned Dec. 24, 1777

3    Captain John McDonell - commissioned Aug. 1, 1778

4    Captain Peter Ten Broeck - commissioned May 4, 1778

5    Captain Peter Hare - commissioned Feb. 8, 1779

6    Captain George Dame - commissioned Nov. 11, 1779

7    Captain Andrew Thompson - commissioned Dec. 25, 1779 - drowned 1781

8    Captain Barent Frey - commissioned Oct. 2, 1780

9    Captain John McKinnon - commissioned Jan. 1, 1781

10   Captain Daniel Servos

11   Captain Lewis Geneway - commissioned Sept. 17, 1781

12   Captain Andrew Bradt - commissioned Sept. 17, 1781

13   Captain-Lieutenant Benjamin Pawling (commanded Lt-Col. John Butler's 10th company of which Butler as nominal commander)

## ENDNOTES

1.Janice Potter-MacKinnon, *While the Women Only Wept: Loyalist Refugee Women in Eastern Ontario* (Montreal & Kingston: McGill-Queen's University Press, 1993), 39 - 41.

2.Christopher Moore, *The Loyalists: Revolution, Exile, Settlement* (Toronto: McClelland and Stewart, 1984, 1994), 114;
Wallace Brown, *The Good Americans: The Loyalists in the American Revolution* (New York: William Morrow and Company Inc, 1969) 34.

3.Earle Thomas, *Sir John Johnson Loyalist Baronet* (Toronto: Dundurn Press, 1986), 13 - 24.

4.Potter-MacKinnon, *While the Women Only Wept*, 50 - 51, 55 - 62.

5.Ernest A. Cruikshank, *The Story of Butler's Rangers and the Settlement of Niagara* (Welland: Lundy's Lane Historical Society, 1893, reprint, Owen Sound, Ontario: Richardson, Bond & Wright, 1975), 11 - 12.

6.Isabel Thomspon Kelsay, *Joseph Brant 1743 - 1807: A Man of Two Worlds* (Syracuse: Syracuse University Press, 1984), 149 - 151;
Paul L. Stevens, *A King's Colonel at Niagara 1774 - 1776: Lt. Col. John Caldwell and the Beginnings of the American Revolution on the New York Frontier* (Youngstown, Old Fort Niagara Association, Inc, 1987), 33 - 35.

7.Stevens, *A King's Colonel*, 51 - 53.

8.Barbara Graymont, *The Iroquois in the American Revolution* (Syracuse: University of Syracuse, 1972), 98.

9.*Ibid.*, 99.

10.Kelsay, *Joseph Brant*, 184.

11.Gavin K. Watt, *Rebellion in the Mohawk Valley: The St. Leger Expedition of 1777* (Toronto: Dundurn Press, 2002) 52 - 53.

12. Mike Phifer, 'Campaign to Saratoga', *Military Heritage*. (Volume2 Number 1 Herndon Va.: Sovereign Media, August 2000), 41.

13.Watt, *Rebellion in the Mohawk Valley*, 71.

14. Graymont, *The Iroquois in the American Revolution*, 122 - 123.

15.Christopher Ward, *War of the Revolution Volume II* (New York: The MacMillan Company, 1952), 481.

16.Graymont, *The Iroquois in the American Revolution*, 125.

17.Watt, *Rebellion in the Mohawk Valley*, 123 - 124.

18. Ernest A. Cruikshank (Gavin Watt, ed.), *The King's Royal Regiment of New York. Toronto with the Index, Appendices and a Master Roll* (The Ontario Historical Society, 1931, reprinted 1984), p. 16 - 17.

19. *Ibid.*, 17.

20.Ward, *War of the Revolution*, 484.

21.Watt, *Rebellion in the Mohawk Valley*, 134.

22.*Ibid.*, 134, 366.

23.Cruikshank , *The Story of Butler's Rangers*, 35 - 36.

24. Dale Van Every, *A Company of Heroes* (New York: William Morrow, 1961), 97.

25.Ward, *War of the Revolution*, 485.

26.Kelsay, *Joseph Brant*, 205.

27.Cruikshank, *The King's Royal Regiment of New York*, 18.

28. *Ibid.*,18.

29. Earle Thomas, *Sir John Johnson: Loyalists Baronet* (Toronto: Dundurn Press, 1986), 76.

30.William W. Campbell, *The Border Warfare of New York During the Revolution, or The Annals of Tryon County* (New York: Baker & Scriber, 1844, reprinted Maryland: Heritage Books, 1992), 110.

31.Howard Swigget, *War Out of Niagara: Walter Butler and the Tory Rangers* (New York: Columbia University Press, 1933), 92.

32. *Ibid.*, 95 - 96;
Watt, *Rebellion in the Mohawk Valley*, 238.

33.Cruikshank, *The King's Royal Regiment of New York*, 20.

34.Graymont, *The Iroquois in the American Revolution*, 146 - 147.

35.Cruikshank, *The Story of Butler's Rangers*, p. 37;
Watt, *Rebellion in the Mohawk Valley*, 283 - 284.

36.Graymont, *The Iroquois in the American Revolution*, 157.

37.Kelsay, *Joseph Brant*, 231.

38. Hazel Mathews, *The Mark of Honour* (Toronto: University of Toronto Press, 1965), 49.

39.Swiggett, *War out of Niagara*, 120.

40.Cruikshank, *The Story of Butler's Rangers*, 43.

41.Van Every, *A Company of Heroes*, 154.

42.Cruikshank, *The Story of Butler's Rangers*, 47.

43.Van Every, *A Company of Heroes*, 157.

44.Graymont, *The Iroquois in the American Revolution*, 171.

45.*Ibid.*, 172.

46.Cruikshank, *The Story of Butler's Rangers*, 46 - 50;
Ward, *War of the Revolution*, 629 - 632.

47.Randolph C. Downes, *Council Fires on the Upper Ohio* (University of Pittsburgh Press, 1940), 214.

48. Stevens, *A King's Colonel at Niagara*, 59.

49.Cruikshank, *The Story of Butler's Rangers*, 51.

50. Ernest A. Cruikshank, 'A Memoir of Lieutenant-Colonel John MacDonell, of Glengarry House, the First Speaker of the Legislative Assembly of Upper Canada', *Ontario History*, (Vol. 25 Willowdale: OHS 1925), 20 - 26.

51.Cruikshank, *The Story of Butler's Rangers*, 52 - 55.

52.Graymont, *The Iroquois in the American Revolution*, 179.

53. *Ibid.*, 180 - 182.

54. Swigget, *War out of Niagara*, 143.

55.Graymont, *The Iroquois in the American Revolution*, 184.

56.Kelsay, *Jospeh Brant*, 228 - 229.

57.Cruikshank, 'A Memoir of Lieutenant-Colonel John MacDonell', 28.

58.Kelsay, *Joseph Brant*, 232.

59.Cruikshank, *The Story of Butler's Rangers*, 56.

60.Campbell, *The Border Warfare of New York*, 134 - 148; Swigget, *War out of Niagara*, 149 - 160.

61.Cruikshank, *The Story of Butler's Rangers*, 56.

62.Graymont, *The Iroquois in the American Revolution*, 190.

63. Mathews, *Mark of Honour*, 76 - 77.

64. Colin G. Calloway, *The American Revolution in Indian Country: Crisis and Diversity in Native American Communities* (Cambridge: Cambridge University Press, 1995), 135.

65. Mathews, *Mark of Honour*, 78.

66. Ernest A. Cruikshank, *Records of Niagara: A Collection of Documents Relating to the First Settlement 1778 - 1783* (Niagara-on-the-Lake: Niagara Historical Society, 1927), 9.

67.*Ibid.*, 10.

68.*Ibid.*, 12.

69.Swigget, *War out of Niagara*, 183.

70.Graymont, p. 203.

71.Cruikshank, *The Story of Butler's Rangers*, 64.

72.Swigget, *War out of Niagara*, 191.

73.Cruikshank, 'A Memoir of Lieutenant-Colonel John MacDonell', 29.

74.*Ibid.*, 29 - 30;
Roger G. Swartz, *Fields of Honor: The Battle of Fort Freeland July 28, 1779* (Turbotville, Pennsylvania: Warrior Run/Fort Freeland Heritage Society, 1996), 72 - 73.

75.Cruikshank, 'A Memoir of Lieutenant-Colonel John MacDonell', 30 - 31; Swartz, *Fields of Honor*, 31.

76.Cruikshank, 'A Memoir of Lieutenant-Colonel John MacDonell', 30. Swartz, *Fields of Honor*, 74.

77.*Ibid.*, 45.

78.Allan W. Eckert, *The Wilderness War* (Toronto: Bantam Books, 1982), 427.

79.Cruikshank , *The Story of Butler's Rangers*, 68 - 70.

80.*Ibid.*, 70.

81. Mike Phifer, 'Destruction of the Iroquois Country', *Black Powder Annual 2000* (Union City, TN: Pioneer Press, 2000), 69 - 71.

82.Cruikshank, 'A Memoir of Lieutenant-Colonel John MacDonell', 33.

83.Graymont, *The Iroquois in the American Revolution*, 214.

84.Phifer, 'Destruction of the Iroquois Country', 69 - 71.

85.Ward, *War of the Revolution*, 643.

86.Eckert, *The Wilderness War*, 459 - 460.

87.Phifer, 'Destruction of the Iroquois Country', 69 - 71.

88.*Ibid.*, 69 - 71.

89.*Ibid.*, 69 - 71.

90.Thomas, *Sir John Johnson*, 83 - 84.

91.Cruikshank, *The Story of Butler's Rangers*, 75.

92.Phifer, 'Destruction of the Iroquois Country', 68.

93.Calloway, *The American Revolution in Indian Country*, 139 - 140.

94.Mary Beacock Fryer, *King's Men, Soldier Founders of Ontario* (Toronto: Dundurn Press Limited, 1980), 78;
Cruikshank , *Story of Butler's Rangers*, 78 - 79.

95.Cruikshank, 'A Memoir of Lieutenant-Colonel John Macdonell', 34;
Cruikshank, *The Story of Butler's Rangers*, 78 - 79.

96.Cruikshank , *Records of Niagara*, 20.

97.*Ibid.*, 20 - 21;
Mathews, *Mark of Honour*, 83.

98.Cruikshank, *Records of Niagara*, 19.
Mathews, *Mark of Honour*, 84.

99.Cruikshank, *Records of Niagara*, 28 - 29.

100.Cruikshank , 'A Memoir of Lieutenant-Colonel John MacDonell', 34.

101.*Ibid.*, 34 - 35.

102.Kelsay, *Joseph Brant*, 292 - 293.

103.Cruikshank, *The King's Royal Regiment of New York*, 45.

104.Cruikshank, *The Story of Butler's Rangers*, 82 - 83.

105. Mike Phifer, 'Destruction of the Mohawk Valley' *Muzzleloader* (Vol. XXVI, No. 4 September/October 1999, Texarkana: Scurlock Publishing Company), 46.

106.*Ibid.*, 46.

107.Cruikshank, *The King's Royal Regiment of New York*, 55.

108.Phifer, 'Destruction of the Mohawk Valley', 46.

109.Gavin K.Watt, *The Burnings of the Valleys: Daring Raids from Canada Against the New York Frontier in the Fall of 1780* (Toronto: Dundurn Press, 1997), 168.

110.*Ibid.*, 171.

111.Campbell, *The Border Warfare of New York*, 178.

112.Phifer, 'Destruction of the Mohawk Valley', 46 - 48.

113.Cruikshank, *The King's Royal of Regiment of New York*, 52.

114.Phifer, 'Destruction of the Mohawk Valley', 46 - 48.

115.Cruikshank, *The King's Royal Regiment of New York*, 52;
Phifer, 'Destruction of the Mohawk Valley', 46 - 48.

116.*Ibid.*, 46 - 48.

117.*Ibid.*, 46 - 48.

118. Cruikshank, *The King's Royal Regiment of New York*, 53.

119.*Ibid.*, 53;
Phifer, 'Destruction of the Mohawk Valley', 46 - 48.

120.Cruikshank, *The King's Royal Regiment of New York*, 53.

121.Cruikshank, *The Story of Butler's Rangers*, 85 - 86.

122.Cruikshank, *The King's Royal Regiment of New York*, 53.

123.*Ibid.*, 53.

124.Phifer, 'Destruction of the Mohawk Valley', 47.

125.Cruikshank, 'A Memoir of Lieutenant-Colonel John MacDonell', 37.

126.Cruikshank, *The Story of Butler's Rangers*, 86.

127.*Ibid.*, 86 - 87.

128.Watts, *The Burning of the Valleys*, 238.

129.Cruikshank, *The King's Royal Regiment of New York*, 55;
Phifer, 'Destruction of the Mohawk Valley', 47 - 48.

130.Cruikshank, *The Story of Butler's Rangers*, 91.

131.Roger G. Swartz, *Frankstown: Anatomy of an Ambush* (Hockessin,
Delaware; Blue Path Press, 1995), 74 - 92.

132.Van Every, *A Company of Heroes*, 260.

133. Butler's Rangers Website , http://www.iaw.on.ca/-
awoolley/brang/brang.html/

134.Cruikshank, *The Story of Butler's Rangers*, 93 - 94.

135.*Ibid.*, 95.

136.Cruikshank, *Records of Niagara*, 23.

137.Van Every, *A Company of Heroes*, 257 - 258;
Kelsay, *Joseph Brant*, 312.

138.Consul Willshire Butterfield, *History of the Girtys* (Cincinnati: Robert Clarke
& Co., 1890, reprinted Lodi, Ohio: Log Cabin Shop, Inc., 1995), 95 - 96.

139.*Ibid.*, 96 - 97.

140.Cruikshank, *The King's Royal Regiment of New York*, 76 - 80;
Cruikshank , *The Story of Butler's Rangers*, 97 - 99.

141.Cruikshank, *The King's Royal Regiment of New York*, 80.

142.*Ibid.*, 81;
Graymont, *The Iroquois in the American Revolution*, 241.

143.Cruikshank, *The King's Royal Regiment of New York*, 82.

144. *Ibid.*, 82.

145. Mathews, *Mark of Honour*, 75.

146.Cruikshank, *The King's Royal Regiment of New York*, 82.

147.Graymont, *The Iroquois in the American Revolution*, 249.

148.Cruikshank, *The Story of Butler's Rangers*, 103.

149.Cruikshank, *The King's Royal Regiment of New York*, 87.

150.Cruikshank, 'A Memoir of Lieutenant-Colonel John MacDonell', 37 - 38.

151.Downes, *Council Fire on the Upper Ohio*, 272 - 273.

152. Butterfield, *History of the Girtys*, 121.

153. *Ibid.,* 125 - 129.

154. John Bakeless, *Daniel Boone Master of the Wilderness* ( Lincoln: University of Nebraska, 1989, reprint of New York: Morrow, 1939), 273.
Cruikshank, *The Story of Butler's Rangers*, 108.

155.Butterfield, *History of the Girtys*, 144.

156.Blakeless, *Daneil Boone*, 274 - 286.

157.*Ibid.*, 287 - 303;
Butterfield, *History of the Girtys*, 147 - 149.

158.Cruikshank, *The Story of Butler's Rangers*, 108.

159.Cruikshank, *The King's Royal Regiment of New York*, 102;
Thomas, *Sir John Johnson*, 98.

160.Calloway, *The American Revolution in Indian Country*, 151 - 153;
Robert S. Allen, *His Majesty's Indian Allies*, (Toronto: Dundurn Press, 1992), 55 - 56;
Carl Benn, *The Iroquois in the War of 1812* (Toronto: University of Toronto, 1998), 19 - 20.

161.Cruikshank, *The Story of Butler's Rangers*, 112.

# BIBLIOGRAPHY:

Allan, Robert S. *His Majesty's Indian Allies*. Toronto: Dundurn Press, 1992.

Arnow, Harriette Simpson. *Seedtime on the Cumberland*. Lincoln: University of Nebraska Press, 1960.

Bakeless, John. *Daniel Boone Master of the Wilderness*. Lincoln: University of Nebraska, 1989 (1939).

Benn, Carl. *The Iroquois in the War of 1812*. Toronto: University of Toronto, 1998.

Bond, Major C.C. J. 'The British Base at Carleton Island', *Ontario History* Vol. LII No.1 Ontario Historical Society, March 1960.

Brown, Wallace. *The Good Americans: The Loyalists in the American Revolution*. New York: William Morrow and Company Inc, 1969.

Butterfield, Consul Willshire. *History of the Girtys*. Cincinnati: Robert Clarke & Co., 1890 (reprinted Lodi, Ohio: Log Cabin Shop, Inc., 1995.).

Calloway, Colin G. *The American Revolution in Indian Country: Crisis and Diversity in Native American Communities*. Cambridge: Cambridge University Press, 1995.

Campbell, William W. *The Border Warfare of New York During the Revolution, or The Annals of Tryon County*. New York: Baker & Scriber, 1844 (reprinted Maryland: Heritage Books, 1992).

Cruikshank, Ernest (Gavin Watt, ed.). *The King's Royal Regiment of New York*. Toronto: The Ontario Historical Society, 1931. (Reprinted 1984).

Cruikshank, Ernest. *The Story of Butler's Rangers and the Settlement of Niagara*. Welland: Lundy's Lane Historical Society, 1893. (Reprint, Owen Sound, Ontario: Richardson, Bond & Wright, 1975. Owen Sound, Ontario: Richardson, Bond & Wright, 1975.

Cruikshank, Ernest. *Records of Niagara: A Collection of Documents Relating to the First Settlement 1778 - 1783*. Niagara-on-the-Lake: Niagara Historical Society, 1927.

Doddridge, Joseph. *The Settlement and Indian Wars of the Western Parts of Virginia and Pennsylvania, 1763-1783*. Bowie, Maryland: Heritage Books Inc., 1988.

Downes, Randolph C. *Council Fires on the Upper Ohio*. University of Pittsburgh Press, 1940.

Draper, Lyman C. (Belue, Ted Franklin editor). *The Life of Daniel Boone*. Mechanicsburg, Pennsylvania: Stackpole Books, 1998.

Eckert, Allan W. *The Frontiersmen*. New York: Bantam Books, 1970.

Eckert, Allan W. *The Wilderness War*. New York: Bantam Books, 1982.

Eckert, Allan W. *A Sorrow in Our Heart*. New York: Bantan Books, 1992.

Fryer, Mary Beacock. *King's Men, Soldier Founders of Ontario*. Toronto: Dundurn Press Limited, 1980.

Furneaux, Rupert. *Saratoga: The Decisive Battle*. London: George Allen &Unwin Ltd, 1971.

Graymont, Barbara. *The Iroquois in the American Revolution*. Syracuse: University of Syracuse, 1972.

Harkness, John Graham. *Stormont, Dundas and Glengarry, A History, 1784-1945*. Ottawa: Mutual Press Limited, 1946.

Hubbard, J. Niles. *Sketches of Border Adventures in The Life and Times of Major Moses Van Campen*. Jersey Shore: Zebrowski Historical Services and Publishing Co., 1992.

Kelsay, Isabel Thomspon, *Joseph Brant 1743 - 1807: A Man of Two Worlds*. Syracuse: Syracuse University Press, 1984.

Kenton, Edna. *Simon Kenton: His Life and Period 1755 - 1836*. Salem, New Hampshire: Ayer Company, Publishers, Inc., 1990.

Kingsford, William. *The History of Canada* Vol. VI. Toronto, Dominion of Canada:Rowsell & Hutchison, 1893.

LaCrosse Jr., Richard B. *The Frontier Rifleman: His Arms, Clothing, and Equipment During the Era of the American Revolution, 1760 - 1800*. Union City, Tennessee: Pioneer Press, 1989.

Lobdell, Jared C. Editor. *Indian Warfare in Western Pennsylvania and North West Virginia at the Time of the American Revolution*. Bowie, Maryland: Heritage Books Inc., 1992.

Mathews, Hazel. *The Mark of Honour*. Toronto: University of Toronto Press, 1965.

Mathews, Hazel. *Frontier Spies: The British Secret Service, Northern Department during the Revolutionary War*. Fort Myers, Florida: Hazel Mathews, 1971.

Moore, Christopher. *The Loyalists*. Toronto: McClelland and Stewart Inc., 1984.

Potter-MacKinnon, Janice. *While the Women Only Wept: Loyalist Refugee Women in Eastern Ontario*. Montreal & Kingston: McGill-Queen's University Press, 1993.

Stevens, Paul L. *A King's Colonel at Niagara 1774 - 1776: Lt. Col. John Caldwell and the Beginnings of the American Revolution on the New York Frontier.* Youngstown, NY: Old Fort Niagara Association Inc, 1987

Stokesbury, James L. *A Short History of the American Revolution.* New York: William Morrow and Company, Inc., 1991.

Swartz, Roger G. *Frankstown: Anatomy of an Ambush.* Hockessin, Delaware: Blue Path Press, 1995.

Swartz, Roger G. *Fields of Honor: The Battle of Fort Freeland July 28, 1779.* Turbotville, Pennsylvania: Warrior Run/Fort Freeland Heritage Society, 1996.

Swigget, Howard. *War Out of Niagara: Walter Butler and the Tory Rangers.* New York: Columbia University Press, 1933.

Talman, James S. (Editor). *Loyalist Narratives from Upper Canada.* Toronto: The Champlain Society, 1946.

Thomas, Earle. *Sir John Johnson Loyalist Baronet.* Toronto: Dundurn Press, 1986.

Van Every, Dale. *A Company of Heroes.* New York: William Morrow, 1962.

Ward, Christopher. *War of the Revolution* Volume I & II.. York: The MacMillan Company, 1952.

Watt, Gavin K. *Rebellion in the Mohawk Valley: The St. Leger Expedition of 1777.* Toronto: Dundurn Press, 2002.

Watt, Gavin K. *The Burning of the Valleys: Daring Raids from Canada Against the New York Frontier in the Fall of 1780.* Toronto: Dundurn Press, 1997.

# INDEX

107

108

## ABOUT THE AUTHOR

Mike Phifer works as an historical interpreter at Upper Canada Village which depicts life in the 1860s. Besides his regular job, he is also a freelance historical writer that writes on Canadian and American military and frontier history. His work has appeared in magazines such as *Military Heritage* and *Black Powder Annual.* Writing *Wolves from Niagara* has been of special interest to him as much of his ancestry comes from the Mohawk Valley, where the Rangers waged part of their war. His ancestors include both Rangers and Patriots.

```
* 9 7 8 0 7 8 8 4 4 3 1 9 0 *
```